Behind the Scenes at the Museum

adapted by
Bryony Lavery

from the novel by Kate Atkinson

THEATRE ROYAL YORK

Theatre Royal Company presents
the world stage premiere of

Behind the Scenes at the Museum

adapted by
Bryony Lavery

from the novel by Kate Atkinson

26 October–18 November 2000

York Citizens' Theatre Trust
Chairman: The Very Rev. Raymond Furnell
Vice Chair: Sue Morris

David Brooks, Gillian Cruddas, David Dickson,
Tricia Ellison, Cllr Steve Galloway,
Cllr Janet M Looker, Adam Tomlinson,
Cllr Peter Vaughan, Alan Vincent,
Cllr C Waite, Tina Wright.
Company Secretary: Cllr Janet M Looker

Trustees of the Theatre Royal Restoration Appeal
Miss D M Hodgson, Prof P Nuttgens,
Mrs B Saville, Cllr C Waite, Mr K Wood (*Chairman*)

Cast
in order of appearance

Ruby	**Katherine Dow Blyton**
Dr Hertzmark, *a psychologist*	**Olwen May**
Bunty, *Ruby's mother*	**Meriel Scholfield**
George, *Ruby's father*	**Mark Stratton**
Gillian, *Ruby's sister*	**Emma Ashton**
Patricia, *Ruby's sister*	**Joanne Heywood**
Nell, *Ruby's grandmother*	**Adele Salem**
Albert, *Nell's brother*	**Stewart Quayle**
Jack, *Albert's friend*	**Julian Kay**
Musical Director, Cellist	**Christopher Madin**
Harpist	**Anna Christensten**
Flautist	**Richard Ingamells**

Other parts played by members of the company

Director	**Damian Cruden**
Designer	**Karen Hood**
Lighting Designer	**Richard G Jones**
Musical Director/Composer	**Christopher Madin**
Sound Designer	**Matt Savage**
Deputy Stage Manager	**Julie Wyman**

(with particular responsibility for this production)

There will be one interval of fifteen minutes

The Sign Language Interpreted performance
for deaf people on Tuesday 14 November
will be by Steven Conlon

The Audio Described performances
for visually impaired people on Friday 17 November
at 8 pm and Saturday 18 November at 4 pm
will be by Jacqui Taylor and John Fletcher

KATE ATKINSON

Kate Atkinson was born in York and now lives in Edinburgh. She studied English Literature at Dundee University and began writing in 1981, producing numerous short stories and winning several prizes, including the Ian St James Award. In 1995 she won the Whitbread Book of the Year Award for her first novel, *Behind the Scenes at the Museum*, beating off competition from Salman Rushdie and Roy Jenkins. *Behind the Scenes at the Museum* also went on to win the Boeker Prize in South Africa and the Livre Book of the Year in France. In the UK it spent more than a year in the UK top 20 paperback bestseller lists and has been translated into 15 languages. To date it has sold over 500,000 copies in the UK.

Her second novel, *Human Croquet*, was published in 1997 to wide critical acclaim in the UK and abroad. It was a *Sunday Times* bestseller in paperback and the UK edition has sold 300,000 copies to date.

Her most recent book, *Emotionally Weird*, published in March, was also a *Sunday Times* bestseller. The paperback version will be out in 2001.

In 1996 Kate wrote an original short play, *Nice*, for the Traverse Theatre, Edinburgh. It was subsequently staged in Paris. Her first full-length play, *Abandonment*, sold out at the Traverse Theatre during this year's Edinburgh Festival.

Kate has also written for a number of magazines and newspapers including the *Scotsman*, *The Observer*, *New Statesman* and *Scotland on Sunday*.

BRYONY LAVERY

Bryony Lavery's plays include *Helen and Her Friends* (1978), *Bag* (1979), *The Family Album (1980)*, *Calamity* (1983), *Origin Of The Species* (1984), *Witchcraze* (1985), *Her Aching Heart* (Pink Paper Play of the Year, 1991), *Kitchen Matters* (1990), *Nothing Compares to You* (1995), *Ophelia* (1996), *Goliath* (1997) and *Frozen* (1998), which won both the TMA Best New Play 1998 and the Eileen Anderson Central Television Award for Best Play of 1998.

For five years she was Artistic Director of Les Oeufs Malades. She was joint Artistic Director of Gay Sweatshop from 1989 to 1991 and a Tutor in Playwriting on the MA Playwriting Course at Birmingham University for three years. She was Resident Playwright at the Unicorn Theatre for Children, 1986-7, and her work for children includes *The Zulu Hut Club* (1983), *Sore Points* (1985), *Madagascar* (1987), *The Dragon Wakes* (1988) and *Down Among the Minibeasts* (1996), which was nominated for Best Children's Play Writers Guild Awards 1996. Her cabaret work includes *Time Gentlemen Please* (1978), *Female Trouble* (1981), *More Female Trouble* (1982) and *The Wandsworth Warmers* (1984). She has appeared in all five of the legendary Drill Hall pantomimes and co-written two of them, *Peter Pan* (1991) and *The Sleeping Beauty* (1992)

Her extensive work for BBC includes the groundbreaking *Revolting Women* for BBC2, adaptations of *Wuthering Heights*, *Lady Audley's Secret* and *A High Wind In Jamaica* for the Classic Serial, and original plays *The Smell of Him*, *The Twelve Days of Christmas*, *Velma and Therese*, *No Joan of Arc* and *Woman of Ice* for Radio 4.

Recent work includes *Shot Through The Heart*, a site-specific large-cast multi-media piece performed at Ludlow Castle, Shropshire in July 2000; *Illyria*, a new play which opened August 2000 at ACT in San Francisco; and an adaptation of *Behind the Scenes at the Museum* for BBC Radio 4. Her biography of *Tallulah Bankhead* was published in 1999 and her play *More Light* was published in October 2000.

She is currently working on *The Opera Companion* for Salibury Playhouse, *The Easter Parade* for Birmingham Rep and *Smoke* for the New Victoria Theatre, Stoke-on-Trent. She is developing a film, *Who Killed Josie O'Dwyer?* and a series, *Girls,* for television. Her play *A Wedding Story* opened at Birmingham in October.

She is an Honorary Doctor of Arts at De Montfort University.

EMMA ASHTON

Originally from Pudsey in West Yorkshire, Emma trained at the University of Hertfordshire, gaining a BA Hons in Performing Arts. Her theatre work includes Mandy in *Out of Their Heads* (Pilot Theatre Company); Lisa in *Crush* (Red Ladder Theatre Company) and Myra in *Ian And Myra* (Durham Theatre Company, Northern Stage). Most recently Emma completed roles in *Behind the Scenes at the Museum* and *Poppy Q* for BBC Radio and she can soon be seen in an episode of *North Square* (Channel 4). Emma is delighted to be working in Yorkshire at the Theatre Royal.

KATHERINE DOW BLYTON

Katherine graduated from Bretton Hall College in 1986. She last appeared at the Theatre Royal as Emelia in *Othello*, and other productions here have included *Bedevilled*, *Turn of the Screw*, *Having a Ball*, *Gargling With Jelly* and *Habeas Corpus*. Katherine has toured with Hull Truck and Compass Theatre Company and has also worked at Harrogate Theatre, Chester Gateway, The Customs House and The Roses Theatre, Tewkesbury. Her television work includes *Coronation Street*, *Emmerdale*, *At Home with the Braithwaites*, *The Cops*, *Where the Heart Is*, *Lost for Words*, *Hollyoaks*, *Stone Scissors Paper*, *Hetty Wainthropp*, *Out of the Blue*, *Common as Muck*, *Cardiac Arrest*, *Band of Gold* and *Cracker*. Katherine also appeared in the film *Brassed Off* and can be seen later this year in the new television series *North Square*. She played Ruby in the Radio 4 production of *Behind the Scenes at the Museum* and is delighted to be recreating the role on stage.

JOANNE HEYWOOD

Born in York, Joanne made her professional debut at the Theatre Royal in *Jack and the Beanstalk* and has since returned to play Dandini in *Cinderella*, Cecily Pigeon in *The Odd Couple* and Lady Capulet in *Romeo and Juliet*. Other theatre work includes the world stage premières of *High Society* and *Scrooge The Musical* and national tours of *Hindle Wakes* and *The Man Mostly Likely To . . .* Her television work includes two series of *First of the Summer Wine*, playing Dilys, two series of *Grace and Favour* as Miss Lovelock, *Brush Strokes, The Brittas Empire, Coronations Street, The New Statesman* and *Peak Practice* with episodes of *Heartbeat* and *Kiss Me Kate* to be shown this Autumn season. Joanne is delighted to be staying on in York to play Dick Whittington in this year's pantomime.

JULIAN KAY

Julian was born and bred in York. He has a degree in Drama and Theatre Arts from Birmingham University and he trained at Guildford School of Acting. His previous work here at the Theatre Royal includes Scratch in *Old Mother Milly* and Les in *Bouncers*. His other theatre work includes *Hot Seat* (Cambridge) and Terry Johnson's production of *Living Together* (Birmingham). His recent television work includes numerous appearances as Robert Preston (Tracy Barlow's husband) in *Coronation Street*, two series of *Dangerfield* as PC Tom Allen, *Coming Home, Peak Practice* and *Emmerdale*. Julian has been something of a one-man marketing machine this year, having been involved in commercials for Scottish bacon, designer footwear and no less than three High Street banks!

OLWEN MAY

Olwen was seen at the Theatre Royal earlier this year playing Anna in *Closer*. Her other theatre work includes *Comedy of Errors* (Duke's Theatre, Lancaster); *The Mikado* (Bolton Octagon); *All My Sons* (Plymouth Theatre Royal); *A Midsummer Night's Dream* and *The Trial* (Contact Theatre, Manchester); *The Crucible* (West Yorkshire Playhouse); *A Doll's House* and *Angels in America* (Library Theatre, Manchester). Her television work includes *The Bill, Doctors, Slug* and *City Central* (BBC); *This Is Personal, A Touch of Frost, Always and Everyone, The Trial of Lord Lucan* and *Coronation Street* (Granada). Her films include *Seeing Red, God on the Rocks* and *My Son the Fanatic*.

STEWART QUAYLE

Stewart had his first taste of acting as a member of the Crucible Youth Theatre in Sheffield. He then moved to London to train as an actor at Middlesex University and decided to stay in London after graduating. Since then his roles include Goody in *Angels with Vertigo* (Union Chapel, Islington) and in November last year he played Liam in *Personals* (White Bear). Stewart then returned to Sheffield earlier this year for the role of Jez in Judy Marsh's *Not Exactly an Angel* at the Sheffield Crucible Studio.

ADELE SALEM

Adele has played a variety of con-artists, embezzlers and murderesses in television dramas including *Kinsey, Dangerfield, The Bill* and *EastEnders*. She was awful anchorwoman Shona Lincoln on the recent Channel 4 comedy *Focus North*. She has toured extensively with the Women's Theatre Group, Spare Tyre, The Magdalena Project, Paines Plough and The Steve Shill Company. Last year she played Indian courtesan Sultana for The Asian Women's Writers Company, Kali Theatre. Adele is a Tai Chi teacher and leads workshops in creative healing. She trained at the Bristol Old Vic Theatre School; this is her first appearance at the Theatre Royal.

MERIEL SCHOLFIELD

Meriel trained at the Royal Academy of Dramatic Art. Her theatre work includes *Perfect Pitch* (Bolton Octagon); *Mirad a Boy From Bosnia* and *Hitler's Childhood* (Oxford Stage Company); *Twelfth Night, On the Piste, Office Party* (Hull Truck); *To Kill a Mockingbird* and *School for Scandal* (Birmingham Rep Theatre); *Love on the Dole* (Oldham Coliseum); and she has worked with Big Space Productions on an adaptation of *The Oresteia* called *The Killing Floor*, where she played Clytemnestra. Her television work includes *Coronation Street, Heartbeat, Cracker, Seeing Red, Emmerdale, Hollyoaks* and *Holby City* to be screened this winter. Meriel has recorded several plays for Radio 4 and appeared in Kenneth Branagh's film *Frankenstein*. She is very happy to be at the Theatre Royal

MARK STRATTON

Mark has worked at the Stephen Joseph Theatre, Scarborough, Nottingham Playhouse, Oldham Coliseum, Derby Playhouse, Harrogate Theatre, Queen's Theatre, Hornchurch, Palace Theatre, Westcliff and here at the Theatre Royal in *A View from the Bridge*, *Up 'n' Under* and *Having a Ball*. National tours include *Reflected Glory*, *It's a Madhouse*, *Fur Coat and No Knickers* and *Joseph*. He has also appeared at the Ludlow Festival and toured his own one-man show *The Incredible Journey*. On television Mark has appeared in *The Ward*, *Coronation Street*, *Emmerdale*, *The Bill*, *Casualty*, *Watchdog* and *World in Action*. He played Robbie Robinson opposite Anthony Hopkins in the film *Across the Lake*.

ANNA CHRISTENSEN

Anna began her studies in her native New Zealand, gaining two diplomas and a Bachelor of Music degree. After completing an MA at the University of Wales, Cardiff, she returned to New Zealand and the post of Principal Harp with the New Zealand Symphony Orchestra until 1989. Since arriving in Britain, she has established a busy and successful freelance career, playing with many of this country's leading orchestras including the Hallé, R.L.P.O and BBC Scottish Symphony Orchestra. Her work has taken her all over Britain with musicals, ballet and orchestras. She has played at the Proms, the Royal Opera House, Covent Garden, and her playing has featured on several orchestral and solo CDs. Each summer she appears with the Performing Arts Symphony Orchestra presenting concerts in the grounds of stately homes and castles throughout England and Wales.

RICHARD INGAMELLS

Richard began playing the flute aged nine. He spent the early part of his career touring with folk and rock groups. In 1996 Richard began studies with flautist Anna Noakes. In 1998 he recorded his debut album, *Flute Classics*, with pianist Kathron Sturrock. Richard has since played with composers Sir Richard Rodney Bennett and Dave Heath.

His latest album, *Indivisible*, released this October, features specially arranged pieces by composer David Ward Maclean. On 29 November Richard will premiere new pieces by composer Andrew Ladd. He has established an international audience over the internet.

CHRISTOPHER MADIN

Christopher is a northern-based composer and cellist. His most recent work includes *Romeo and Juliet, The Snow Queen, Frog and Toad* and *Tidelines* (Crucible Theatre, Sheffield); *Passion Killers, Up 'n' Under 2, Bouncers* and *Laurel and Hardy* (Hull Truck Theatre); *Act of Faith* (Quandam Theatre Co.) and *Beauty and the Beast* (Chester Gateway); *Miss Julie, A Christmas Carol, Jekyll and Hyde, Electra, A Doll's House, Wind in the Willows, Twelfth Night, She Stoops to Conquer,* and the current tour of *Hard Times*. He was producer on *Carolans Dream* and *Islands,* CDs of 18th-century Celtic harp music, he wrote the music for *Habeas Corpus, Up 'n' Under, Frankenstein, The Snow Queen, Having a Ball, Bouncers, Romeo and Juliet, The Glass Menagerie* and *Othello* here at the Theatre Royal. He has just completed three years as Artist in residence at the University College, Bretton Hall.

DAMIAN CRUDEN

Originally from Scotland, Damian trained at the Royal Scottish Academy of Music and Drama and then worked for Scottish companies such as the Tron and T.A.G. He was Youth Theatre Director at the Liverpool Everyman and Associate Director at Hull Truck. Damian has worked in various theatres throughout the country, including Chester Gateway, Sheffield Crucible, The Customs House and the Queen's Theatre, Hornchurch. Plays directed include *Laurel and Hardy, Bouncers, Up 'n' Under, Happy Jack, As You Like It, House, Off Out, Road Movie, Act of Faith, Two, My Mother Said I Never Should, It's a Girl, Lucky Sods, Beauty and the Beast, Gargling with Jelly, Negative Returns, April in Paris* and *Lonely Hearts*. As the Artistic Director of the Theatre Royal in York, he has directed *Habeas Corpus, Up 'n' Under, Frankenstein,*

The Turn of the Screw, Bedevilled, Man of the Moment, Having a Ball, Bouncers, Beauty and the Beast, Romeo and Juliet, Getting On, Noises Off, Little Shop of Horrors, The Glass Menagerie, Old Mother Milly, Othello, Closer and *A Funny Thing Happened on the Way to the Forum.*

KAREN HOOD

Karen trained in Theatre Design at Trent Polytechnic in Nottingham, graduating in 1986. Earlier this year she designed *Hourglass* by Richard Hurford for the Theatre Royal. She recently worked at the Crucible Theatre in Sheffield where she has designed several productions, amongst these *Chameleon* by Richard Hurford, *After Juliet* by Sharman Macdonald, *Slap* by Lisa Evans and *Bouncers* by John Godber. She has an insatiable passion for travelling to exotic places, and in 1996 she was awarded a scholarship to study Japanese theatre companies, including Theatre Zenshinza, designing *Barefoot Gen* by Keiji Nakazowa. This summer Karen was involved in taking a group of young people from Sheffield to Kijo in Japan for a cultural exchange trip.

RICHARD G JONES

Richard's lighting design work includes designs for the Swan Theatre, Worcester; Everyman Theatres, both in Cheltenham and Liverpool; Library Theatre, Manchester; The Watermill Theatre, Newbury; Guildford School of Acting, Norwich Playhouse, The new Culture and Congress Centre, Lucerne; and The Theatre on the Lake, Keswick. Richard's work here at the Theatre Royal includes *A Funny Thing Happened on the Way to the Forum, Closer, Othello, Old Mother Milly, The Glass Menagerie, The Cherry Orchard, Little Shop of Horrors, Noises Off, Getting On, Romeo and Juliet, Beauty and the Beast, Gargling with Jelly, Bouncers, Man of the Moment, The Turn of the Screw, Bedevilled, Into the Woods, Macbeth* and *The 1996 York Cycle of Mystery Plays.* Richard has recently lit a touring production of *Carmen* for the Watermill Theatre, Newbury, the summer season for The Theatre on the Lake, Keswick and he is working on plans for the Salvation Army Christmas Spectacular in London.

Behind the Scenes at the Museum

adapted by
Bryony Lavery

from the novel by
Kate Atkinson

faber and faber

First published in 2000
by Faber and Faber Limited
3 Queen Square, London WC1N 3AU
Published in the United States by Faber and Faber Inc.
an affiliate of Farrar, Straus and Giroux Inc., New York

Typeset by Country Setting, Kingsdown, Kent CT14 8ES
Printed in England by Intype London Ltd

All rights reserved

Copyright © Bryony Lavery, 2000

The right of Bryony Lavery to be identified as author
of this work has been asserted in accordance with
Section 77 of the Copyright, Designs and Patents Act 1988

All rights whatsoever in this work, amateur or professional,
are strictly reserved. Applications for permission for
any use whatsoever including performance rights must be
made in advance, prior to any such proposed use,
to Peters, Fraser & Dunlop, Drury House, 34–43 Russell Street,
London WC2B 5HA. No performance may be given
unless a licence has first been obtained.

*This book is sold subject to the condition that it shall not, by
way of trade or otherwise, be lent, resold, hired out or otherwise
circulated without the publisher's prior consent in any form of
binding or cover other than that in which it is published and
without a similar condition including this condition being
imposed on the subsequent purchaser*

A CIP record for this book
is available from the British Library

ISBN 0–571–20911–4

2 4 6 8 10 9 7 5 3 1

Characters

in order of appearance

Ruby
Dr Hertzmark, a psychologist
Bunty, Ruby's mother
George, Ruby's father
Gillian, Ruby's sister
Patricia, Ruby's sister
Nell, Ruby's grandmother
Albert, Nell's brother
Jack, Albert's friend

Other parts are played by members of the company

Some Notes

We are in the Lost Property Cupboard . . . the great metaphysical one which surrounds us all and where it is possible to reach the bottom and find lost memories and then everything will be all right.

This particular Lost Property Cupboard is full of ghosts, props, people . . . and particularly . . . the past of a York family called Lennox.

The corporeal characters in this story have only at best a dim sense of this Lost Property Cupboard . . . until they die, become ghosts . . . and then things become much clearer to them. Have compassion, they are Only Human. They have, however, the capacity to form themselves physically into family clumps, groups, lines, clusters, to tell a story . . .

All occupants are infinitely theatrical about creating poignant, immediate scenes as required. Realities can bleed into one another . . . after all, it's family . . . characters from different time zones can observe other scenes at will.

Remember . . . the past is a cupboard full of light and all you have to do is find the key that opens the door . . .

We, the fortunate audience, are entirely aware of the Lost Property Cupboard and its occupants. For one magical night, we can see everything . . .

Bryony Lavery,
October 2000

*This play is laid out to help the actors find
the true rhythms of dramatic speech.*

*None of the characters speak in sentences
or observe punctuation or breathe at the right time.*

> Because   often
> They are in   torment.

*The short lines, the spaces within or between lines,
are there on purpose to indicate the subtext and
to help the performer to find the physical
and emotional journey within a speech.*

*I hope the reader will observe the deliberate
eccentricities of my punctuation . . .*

Act One

ONE
HELP

Darkness.

Ruby
  Help!
  Anybody?
  Please!!!!

  Is anybody there?
  there's blackness
  more blackness
  blackness like a woolly shroud
  blackness that's trying to get inside me

  I'm being buried alive

  Help me!

TWO
DR HERTZMARK GETS BUSY

Lights on Ruby standing, dazed. A kind, intelligent, middle-aged German woman . . .

Hertzmark
  Hello Ruby . . .
  I'm Dr Hertzmark
  and I'd like to help you . . .
  is that alright?

Ruby
  Yes.

Hertzmark
Do you want to lie down?

Ruby
Here?

Hertzmark
Yes.

Hertzmark
Good.
Wrap yourself in this nice blue blanket . . . ?
Yes . . .
and just
. . . breathe . . .

Now then, Ruby . . .
I want you to imagine that
you're wrapped
safe
in all the colours of the rainbow

Ruby
Red
for Ruby.

Hertzmark
Red for Ruby   good
and now
you're a clever girl . . .
start counting down from ten . . .

Ruby
Ten
nine
eight
seven
six
five
four
three

Hertzmark
>Good girl.
>
>Ruby
>you are quite safe
>nothing can harm you
>and you are allowed to remember
>everything . . .
>
>*Music, surpassingly beautiful, begins . . .*
>
>We live in a museum, Ruby . . .
>and behind the scenes . . .

Hertzmark
>It's full of ghosts . . .
>
>you can hear them if you listen hard . . .
>all the ghosts of York . . .
>
>*A sound of water and rowing . . .*
>
>The splash of water from Viking oars . . .
>
>*A sound of horses hooves on cobbles . . . hounds baying . . .*
>
>The Harrogate Tally-Ho rattling over cobblestones . . .
>
>*A hunting horn, then marching feet . . .*
>
>The Roman Legion that conquered
>the North march up this street outside . . .
>
>Can you hear them?

Ruby
>Yes.

Hertzmark
>Dick Turpin was hung a few streets away
>
>*A scream, a crowd roars . . .*
>
>Go where you need to go, Ruby,
>visit the ghosts who will help you . . .

Some family ghosts arrive, watch Ruby as . . .

Ruby
    Down
    down
    down (*not nice*)
    hurtling through space and time and darkness!

Hertzmark
    The Past, Ruby . . .
    is a cupboard of light . . .
    and all you have to do is to find
    the key that opens the door . . .

    Ghosts attend, help, as . . .

Ruby
    I accelerate (*stressful, uncomfortable*)
    down towards the stars twinkling
    at the end of the world . . .
    I'm starting to float (*it's better*)

    I can see strange objects in the darkness . . .

    I'm floating with them!

    Bubbling   plopping   sonic   lunar . . .

    We're all getting faster . . .

    whizzing along now!
    incredible speed!

    Hurtling!
    Shooting!
    Firing!
    Exploding!
    I
    I
    I
    I . . .

THREE
CONCEPTION

Ruby
>I exist!

Alice activates the clock . . .

>I am conceived to the chimes of midnight
>on great-grandmother Alice's clock . . .

Chimes . . . ghosts open, say, a large drawer somewhere, revealing George and Bunty having marital sex . . .

Ruby
>I'm begun on the first stroke

Sound of sexual exertion as . . .

George
>Yes oh yes . . .

Ruby
>and finished on the last.

And it's over.

George
>Yessss!

Ruby
>my father rolls off my mother
>plunges into a dreamless sleep

He does . . . wonderful snoring . . .

>thanks to five pints of John Smith's.
>
>My mother's pretending to be asleep
>
>my father never lets that put him off

My father's name is George
My mother's name is Berenice
but everyone always calls her Bunty

Bunty

...In my dreams I'm Vivien Leigh...
pirhouetting in front of a cheval mirror
dark
mysterious
with ruby-red lipstick
and
possibilities!...
But when I wake up
when I wake up...
Don't wake him
don't wake him I don't want to endure that
more than once in twelve hours!

George's snores whistle and syncopate...

Ruby

My conception has left Bunty
feeling irritated...

Alarm clock...day...

Bunty

Shut up!

Alarm clock does.

Hertzmark

An emotion with which she's very comfortable...

Bunty

I'm very disappointed by marriage
it's failed to change my life in any way
except by making it worse!

She gets up...goes downstairs...

Why didn't anyone tell me
What it would be like?
The babies!
The work!
The broken nights!
The power struggles . . .
The labour pains!
At least that's all over with . . .

Ruby
Surprise!

Bunty
Tea!

Makes tea . . . cooker . . . pot . . .

I could have married a GI!
If he hadn't had his foot blown off
fooling around with that landmine . . .
Anything for a lark, those Yanks!

Small, stout party bumps downstairs . . .

Ruby
Here's Gillian!

Hertzmark
Gillian?

Ruby (*awful loss*)
My sister . . .
all arms and soft legs
and sweet bedtime smells . . .

Gillian tries to climb up Bunty . . .

Gillian
mmmmmmu . . . ummmmmm . . .

Bunty
Get down, Gillian.

Mummy's thinking . . .
The war was a big disappointment . . .
I should have been in a war where
I manned searchlights
loaded ack-acks
where I was resourceful
and beautiful . . .
and plucky! . . .
Where
'String of Pearls' played
endlessly
and a succession of
unbelievably handsome officers
whirled me off into another life . . .

Porridge
Toast
Eggs.

A ladylike belch . . .

Bit liverish this morning.
If he wants anything he can get it
himself.
Bowl for Gillian.
Bowl for me.
. . . I think I can manage a bit of porridge . . .

Sound of young party, with attitude, arriving downstairs . . .

Bowl for Patricia . . .

Ruby (*hurting*)
Patricia!

Patricia
I don't like porridge.

Bunty
Pardon me?

Patricia
I don't like porridge.

Bunty
Well . . . I don't like children,
so that's too bad for you, isn't it?

A shop door dings. A door opens.

The sound of . . . a parrot, puppies yelping, kittens mewing, budgerigars fluttering and chirping . . .

Ruby (*joy*)
Oh!

Hertzmark
Where are you now?

Ruby
The Shop!
Our Shop!
Our Pet Shop!
There's the Parrot!

Parrot speaks loud offended 'Parrot'.

George
Just slipping out.
Mind the shop, Bunt!

Ruby and **Bunty**
He's always slipping out!

Bunty
Bunt?
He might at least ask!
Cuttlefish is fourpence . . .
I'm a wife and mother!
Not a shop assistant!

The budgerigars are two and sixpence
per breeding pair . . .

Bunty
Slipping out?   Where to?
No, we're out of the cheap Hamster Food!

You kids get bloody dressed!
We've got to see Grandma!
And I'm not feeling too . . .

Ruby
Pleased with what's inside her . . .

nor me . . .

Bunty vomits . . .

Bunty
Why am I feeling sick . . .?

Ruby
Why do I have this strange feeling . . .
as if my shadow's stitched to my back . . .?
as if there's someone else in there with me . . .?

Nell (*approaching*)
Where are you?
Where are you?

Hertzmark
We seem to have left Conception.
Who's this, Ruby?

Ruby
It's Grandma.

Nell
Is this the Lake District?
Am I on my honeymoon?
Who did I marry?

Ruby
> She lives with us.
> She had Old Timer's . . .

Hertzmark
> Alzheimer's . . .

Ruby
> disease . . .

Hertzmark
> You start to heal the child . . .
> and ten to one . . . the whole bloody family
> wants to be healed too!

Ruby
> But . . . she's just *died* . . .

Nell
> Mother?
> Lillian?

Hertzmark
> The newly-dead take a bit to find their feet . . .
> Who are you looking for, sweetheart?

Nell
> My sister!
> Lillian!

FOUR
SISTERS, BROTHERS AND FAMILIES

Great War music . . . Lillian appears . . .

Lillian
> Nell?

Nell
> Lillian!

They meet and greet each other ecstatically as . . .

Rachel
You Two!
Neither of you seem capable
of catching a husband
and one day I'll die
and you'll be on your own!

Lillian
If only . . .

Nell
Oh God, why take our mother and
leave her?

Hertzmark
I'm confused . . .

Ruby and **Nell**
Well, when Great Grandmother (my mother) Alice
went off with the French photographer . . .
Rachel came to look after us/them . . .

Rachel
They were very dirty, peevish,
unmanageable children . . .!

Ruby and **Nell**
and she got our Great-grandfather/Father
to marry her . . .

Rachel
The scrubbing I had to do!
The ear-boxing!
The punishments!

Nell and **Lillian**
We really *hate* her!

Lillian
>Maybe we'll find ourselves a soldier . . .

Three World War One soldiers, Frank, Albert and Jack, emerge from a dug-out somewhere as . . .

Nell and **Lillian** (*ecstatic*)
>Albert!!!!!

Albert
>My lovely sisters!

Nell and **Lillian**
>We really *love* him!

Albert waves back as he and other soldiers prepare to have photographs taken . . .

Rachel
>There's always a flock of girls after Albert but *he* never chooses one to be special!

Albert
>I don't think I'll ever get married.

Jack
>I think I will!
>Are those your sisters, then?

Lillian
>That's daft.

Nell
>He'd make a grand husband.

Lillian (*to Nell, whisper*)
>I'd marry him myself.
>If he wasn't my brother.

Albert
>This is Jack Keech. My sisters. Lillian. Nell.

Frank
I'm Frank.

Lillian
Albert looks like an angel . . .
laughing
always laughing

blond curls   baby blue eyes

Albert
My stepmother Rachel. Jack's a chippy.

Frank
I'm Frank.

Nell (*of Jack*)
Lock of dark hair
always falling over his forehead
skin on his arms the colour of polished walnut . . .

Albert
He looks a real toff, eh, Nelly?

Frank
I'm Frank.

Nell
Men usually went for Lillian . . .

Frank
I'm Frank.
Do you fancy a walk?

Lillian
No.

Jack
Do you fancy a walk?

Lillian
No.

Jack
> Do you fancy a walk?

Nell
> Alright.
> I was very lucky to get Jack.

Albert
> Time to go, lads!

They pick up equipment. One last photograph. Albert fools around, arms round Jack, then . . .

Nell (*to Jack*)
> Here's a good luck charm for you.

A rabbit's foot.

Jack
> They should make them standard issue, eh?

Frank
> I'll write.

A lot of complicated kissing. Albert getting most, then Jack, Frank getting none.

Then soldiers march out . . .

Rachel
> He's gone then, has he, the light of your life?

Nell
> Albert!   Jack!   Don't leave me . . .!

She wanders after them . . .

Ruby
> Grandma . . .!

Hertzmark
> Let her wander . . .
> Here is my Lost Property Cupboard

theory of the afterlife . . . when we die we are
taken to the great Lost Property Cupboard
where all the things we have ever lost
have been kept for us . . .
every hairgrip, every button
and pencil, every tooth,
every earring and key
every pin . . .
which part of the cupboard are you
in now, Ruby?

Ruby's body starts contorting . . . a maelstrom of grunts, machines voices as . . .

Ruby
I don't like this
I don't like this one little bit!
Get me out of here somebody quick!

Hertzmark holds her hand as . . .

My frail little skeleton is being crushed!
My tender skin . . . chafed raw
by this . . . sausage-making process
. . . this can't be natural!!!!!

Meanwhile a scene has gathered . . .

Doctor
Get a move on, woman,
I've a bloody dinner party to go to!

Midwife
Push! Push now!

Bunty
I am bloody pushing!

Ruby
Nine months in here's been no picnic!
and . . . recently . . . there's been no

room at all!
I don't care what's out there . . .
it has to be better than this!

Grunts, breathing, pushing . . . from the exterior and interior sides of birth until . . .

Doctor
Hello, what have we here?

Midwife
Snap!

Doctor
Another girl!
Clean her up.

Midwife
Mummy might like a look . . .

Bunty
Looks like a piece of meat.
Take it away.

Midwife
Baby Lennox.

Ruby
She wraps me up
in a white cotton cellular blanket
like a parcel
puts me in a cot.

Sound of newborn babies gruntling . . .

Ruby
Little baby parcels everywhere . . .
I think I just lie there . . .

The nurse appears with another
baby parcel and puts it down in

the empty cot near me . . .
she pins a label on its blanket . . .

Suppose the parcel lost its label
got mixed up . . .?

New-born baby crying . . .

The new baby nexts to me sleeps
peacefully
and I . . .
(*bursts into tears*) Waaaaaaaa!
Waaaaa!   Waaaaaa!

Hertzmark
It's alright, Ruby . . .

Midwife
The little bastard's going to wake them all!

Ruby
Is she taking me to my Mummy?

Midwife
There, you little bastard!

Ruby
It's a little side room . . .
a cupboard really . . .
I spend my first night on earth
in a cupboard.

Poignant baby-in-cupboard music . . .

FIVE
LETTERS HOME

Explosions throughout . . .

Nell
We had letters.

Nell
We never had so many letters in our lives . . .

Albert
. . . I'm missing home cooking and picking
up a bit of the lingo . . .

Lillian (*to Rachel*)
He says he's missing home
cooking but he's picked up a bit of the lingo . . .

Albert
The lads are a grand lot
and we're kept very busy . . .

Soldiers dodge sniper fire, etc, . . . as . . .

Jack
I'm thinking about you and thank you
for your letters . . .

Nell and **Lillian** (*softly*)
I'm thinking about you and thank
you for your letters . . .

Nell
We even got letters from Frank . . .

Frank
Thank you for the grand cup of tea . . .
in the tea service with the gold rim . . .

and the bread and jam . . .
the water here is chlorinated . . .

Nell
Of course he's got no one to write to . . .

Lillian
They never write about skirmishes or
battles or whatnot . . .

Huge explosion . . . all soldiers flatten . . .

Albert
Well . . . the Battle of Ypres is over now
and we are all very glad . . .

Rachel
It must be dreadful!
All that Froggy Food!

Soldiers
Dear God . . .
please don't let me die . . .

Lillian
Let me read Albert's letter again.
Oh . . . and Jack's . . .

Nell
It's not so bad, lads.
Better than getting old and living
with your daughter!

SIX
CORONATION DAY

Nell joins a gathering Coronation Day celebration . . .

Bunty
>It's Coronation Day.
>I've done some baking . . .

Nell
>It's better than life . . .

Bunty
>'The good cook knows that nothing will repay
>her skill so well as attractive cakes, whether
>nut brown from the oven or daintily decorated . . . '
>*The Parkinson Gas Stove Cook Book* . . .
>my bible . . .

Nell
>Hallelujah!

Bunty
>So . . . scones . . . Ham Sandwiches, Coconut
>Madeleines, Lamingtons, Little Caramel
>Pastries '*Very Special!*', Piccaninnies,
>'*From Australia!!!*', Dago Cakes . . .
>I've saved butter . . . it's slightly rancid . . . but . . .

Coronation Day invitees arrive as . . .

>Auntie Gladys has brought a big pork pie
>Auntie Babs two fruit flans, one of overlapping
>tinned peaches and maraschino cherries,
>one Bartlett pears and grapes . . .
>perfectly flawless circles . . .

Everybody
>Oooh!

Bunty
>Everybody's *that* impressed
>I don't think she's got enough to *do*
>*Men* are all just drinking
>and there's too many children . . .

Nell
>Can I do anything?

Bunty
>Just sit down, Mother.

Ted
>Pretty Polly! Pretty Polly!
>Ouch . . . Christ!

Parrot parrots indignantly . . .

Ruby
>There's Bunty and George and Patricia and Gillian and me of course but I just go dotty dotty dotty . . . and Clifford and Ted and Bill and Grandma and Eliza and Lucy Vida and Adrian and . . .

Music . . .

>somebody else . . . but I can't remember . . .

>We're all very proud of our new television . . .

All
>Oooh!

Dimbleby
>'The young queen is now being girded with the sword . . . '

Gillian (*singing*)
>On the good ship Lollipop
>it's a short walk to the candy shop!

Bunty
   Shut up, Gillian

Patricia (*reading*)
   'The Coronation signifies an act of beautiful symbolism, the power of the State placed at the service of God . . . '

Bunty
   Shut up, Patricia.

Ruby
   Dotty dotty dotty

Bunty
   Shut up, Ruby.

George
   Where does George Fourth come then? in t'order?

Bunty
   Shut up, George.

Clifford
   Well, there was one, two and three . . .

George
   Weren't Queen Anne between three and four?

Bill
   He was that fat git that built Brighton . . .

Aunt Gladys
   He was the one that lost us America. Ay Patricia?

Patricia
   I'm only up to Edward the Second!

Gillian
   On the good ship . . .

Bunty
Shut up, Gillian!

Lucy Vida
Come here, our kid.

Bunty
Patricia, tell everybody what you got
for the Coronation . . .

Patricia
A coronation mug, coronation coins in
a plastic wallet, coronation medal identical
to the one the Queen's going to pin on
Charles' little chest later today . . . coronation
toffees and (*reveal*) The Daily Graphic
Coronation Book for Boys and Girls . . .

Gillian
On the Good Ship . . .

Bunty
Gillian!

Lucy Vida
Never mind, kid . . . I'll teach you the splits later.

Patricia
It's the anointing with the holy oil!

Bunty
Get out of the way, Gillian!
People are trying to watch!

Gladys
That's a lovely television set.

Bunty
Thank you.

Nell
>Nice bit of walnut veneer.
>Jack was a chippy.

Bunty
>Shut up, Mother.

Patricia (*reading*)
>'Now comes the moment for
>which all the peoples of Britain,
>the Commonwealth, and Empire
>have been waiting . . . '

Ted (*touching up Patricia*)
>The Supreme Moment . . .

Patricia
>Get off.

All
>God Save The Queen!

Ruby
>Pas   Gug   Gamma ByebyeShop
>dottydotty mobo . . .
>I had a mobo horse!
>Maybe it's my mobo horse I forgot!

Ted
>Would you little girls like to come
>upstairs for a game?
>
>It's called *Surprise*!!!

Girls (*all crying*)
>*No!!!*

Gillian
>Mine!

Ruby
>Gillian pulls it off me.

Ruby and Gillian cry in stereo . . .

Ruby
I go out in the yard with Teddy . . .

Coronation scene dismantles . . . as . . .

Ruby
Oh!

I left him in the back yard!

That's who I forgot!

And late
late at night
I remember!

I get up
The moon's so bright . . .

A door opens . . . moonlight streams . . .

Ruby
and Daddy's doing something
to an unidentified lady by
the dustbins . . .

George
Oh yes oh yes oh yes . . .

Ruby
and the lady's saying . . .

Lady
Come on, pet, that's the way . . .

Ruby
I suppose I'd better leave Teddy here
till morning . . .
I get in bed with Patricia . . .

Patricia (*reading*)
'You will have to grow up and
when you have left childhood you must
behave as a responsible man or woman.
This may sound rather frightening, but you
know as well as I do that although as a nation
we have sometimes made mistakes
we have never lacked courage . . . '

Ruby turns to where George . . .

George
Yessss!

Lady
Well done, pet!

Ruby and **Patricia**
God Bless The Queen
and God Bless all the peoples of
The United Kingdom.
God Bless Us All.

God Save The Queen plays . . . Albert runs, dodging sniper fire towards . . .

SEVEN
GOODBYE ALBERT

Nell
When Albert comes home on leave . . .

He arrives, exhausted . . .

Rachel
More mouths to feed!

Lillian
We're greedy for him!

Nell
Hang around his neck!

Lillian
Stroke his hair!

They do . . .

Nell
I'm sewing uniforms!

Lillian
I'm a tram conductress!

Albert
I just want to sleep!

He falls asleep . . .

Nell
He wants to sleep all the time!

Lillian
There's fine lines round his eyes . . .

Nell
He won't answer questions!

Albert (*laughing*)
It's like Scarborough!
It's a right Picnic!
It's Champion!

Nell
He's no sooner here

Lillian
Than he's gone!
we wave him off . . .

Nell
We're still standing ten minutes after he's gone . . .

Rachel
He's gone then, has he, the light of your life?

Nell and **Lillian**
Shut up!
Just shut up!

Huge explosion . . . Albert, Frank, Jack . . . trenches somewhere . . .

Frank
It's strange . . .
Albert looks perfectly all right
but he's dead
Jack
is covered in blood from head to foot
he looks like one of the martyrs
of the early church
but he's alive
we all three turn up same dressing station
seems perfectly natural
not strange
but then . . .
I think I'm dead . . . the
only dead person I see all day is Albert . . .

Lillian
I'm taking fares on a tram . . .
the middle of Blossom street and

Cold shiver runs through her . . .

I pull the ticket machine over my head
and . . .

Rings bell . . . leaves machine . . . steps off tram.

passengers watching . . .

I walk up Blossom Street
down Micklegate
then I'm . . .

Running . . .

When I turn into Lowther Street
I see . . .

Nell sitting on a doorstep . . .

Nell
I was sitting stitching uniforms
basement
and . . .

Both sit together, holding hands . . .

Lillian
He's died
just now
didn't he?

Nell
When the telegram came . . .

Rachel (*reading*)
We regret to inform you that
Albert Barker was killed in action on July 1st
1916. The Army Council sends its sympathy . . . '

Nell
we'd been in mourning for a week . . .

Frank
The only mark on him
a line of grease and blood on his
cheek . . .

Jack
and a smile on his face . . .
like a child who's just seen his mother
in the crowd . . .

Frank
you would wonder what had killed him . . .

Jack
>until you lifted him up
>and saw the back of his head was missing . . .

Lillian goes to . . .

Nell
>We'd shared a room . . . me and Lil . . .
>she gets all her stuff . . .
>moves into Albert's bed . . .

Lillian
>I wish we hadn't washed his sheets!

Nell
>Like she was . . . his wife . . .

She wanders off, puzzled, crossing with Bunty . . .

Bunty
>I *miss* the war!
>There was a lot of *men* about then!
>I tried a few . . .
>but the best one was . . .

He appears . . .

>Edmund!
>He was Canadian!
>But so beautiful!
>Standing in his officer's uniform
>his RAF cap pushed to the back of his
>head so you could see how curly his blond hair was . . .
>and grinning
>and saying

Edmund
>Hi.

Bunty
>in a very unEnglish sort of way . . .
>He lived

Edmund
>on a farm!
>smack in the middle of the prairies!

Bunty
>He made me think of a lion . . .
>a great golden-velvet lion . . .
>and his eyes . . .
>they were . . .
>sky blue?
>sea blue?

Edmund
>Ten!
>Gee!
>Gotta go. Curfew!
>(*to us, winking*) Got a girl waiting . . .
>. . . little Irish cutie . . .
>
>*He walks off . . .*

Bunty
>It doesn't matter
>
>he never came back
>
>he was shot down on his next sortie
>
>*Explosions, gunfire as . . .*
>
>and then . . . I settled for George

George
>Can I get you a drink, or what?
>I'm not courting

Bunty
>And I became a wife . . .
>
>and my mother gave me her silver locket . . .
>
>*Nell gives her the silver locket . . .*

Nell
It was your Grandma Alice's
she left it when she ran off . . .
only
your spirits seem so low
considering you're about to get married . . .

Bunty
forget-me-not blue!
. . . that's what they were!

Nell
I lost something in the war

Bunty
I lost something in the war.

It was the chance to be somebody else

Hertzmark
She's sad.

Ruby
I'm sad.

Hertzmark
Why are you sad?

Ruby
I don't know!

Hertzmark
When did you first not know?
Ten
nine
eight
seven
. . .

Music and light and sound turn horribly frightening and upsetting and into . . .

EIGHT
THE NAMING OF THINGS

Ruby sitting holding Teddy.

Ruby
I don't think this is Kansas, Teddy.
But where on earth is it?
What's that you say, Teddy?

Teddy talks . . .

Dewsbury?
Oh God, let him be wrong.
But he's not
this is Dewsbury
Shoddy Capital of the North.

But why?
Why are we in Dewsbury
and worse
not just in Dewsbury
but in the attic bedroom of
number twelve, Mirthroyd Road . . .
the den
the lair
the pod
of the twins from hell
Daisy and Rose

Daisy and Rose arrive . . .

Spooky music . . .

They regard me with solemn little eyes.

Twins
Look at her.

Ruby
>They are perched on the edge of the
>double bed they share

Twins
>This is our bed.
>that's yours.

Ruby
>I am installed on an old camp bed
>
>(*as in . . . 'the very bowels of hell' . . .*)
>
>The guest bed.

Twins
>You're our guest.
>Our mother says 'Be nice to her'

Ruby
>You're not my sisters.

Twins
>We're each other's sister.
>We're twins.

Ruby
>I'm Ruby Lennox.
>
>I have a mother, father
>and sisters . . .
>Are you an alien life force?
>Has your spaceship sucked me up?
>Are you going to conduct
>experiments on me?
>
>They don't talk
>they just look
>they're exactly the same
>except Daisy apparently
>has a freckle under her chin

Daisy
   Look.
   Freckle.

Ruby
   but Rose hasn't.

Rose
   Look.
   No freckle.

Ruby
   Auntie Babs comes in.

Babs
   Well . . . play with your cousin!

Ruby
   Oh God . . . *I'm* their cousin!

Twins
   Do you want to play?
   A game?
   A toy.
   They all belong to us.
   Don't break anything.

Hertzmark
   they have a very limited range of
   facial expressions.

Ruby
   I'm beginning to miss the startling
   variety of emotions that scud like
   clouds across Gillian's face . . .
   or even the sombre, yet subtle
   palette that Patricia draws from . . .

Daisy
   I'm Daisy.

Rose
>I'm Rose.

Twins
>See the freckle?

Ruby
>No.
>You both look exactly the same.

Twins
>Well . . . we're *twins*.
>. . . let's get the Fuzzyfelts.

Ruby
>Why am I here?
>Is this a holiday?
>It doesn't feel like a holiday.
>If I have a quick game of Fuzzyfelts . . .
>will I be allowed home?
>
>My suitcase contains a pair of
>winceyette pyjamas, a pair of
>ruby-red slippers, five pairs of
>knickers . . . a liberty bodice . . .
>
>*Mounting horror . . .*
>
>two viyella blouses, a kilt . . .
>a corduroy pinafore dress, a pair
>of tartan trews, two handknitted
>jumpers . . . a petticoat . . . four
>
>*It gets worse . . .*
>
>pairs of socks plus of course what
>I was wearing when I arrived
>one blue woollen skirt
>
>*And worse . . .*

one yellow jumper one winter coat
one pair gloves,
one scarf one woollen hat
I am clearly here for some time!!!!!!

I clutch Teddy tightly.

Twins
Look at her strangling her Teddy.

Ruby
I have horrible nightmares!

Why am I here?
What have I done?

Hertzmark
You thought you had done something?

Ruby
I don't know!

Hertzmark
No clues?

What do you remember?

Ruby
I've got a croupy cough . . .

Hertzmark
Yes . . . ?

Ruby
And Aunt Babs says . . .

Babs
It's lucky that's all you have . . .

Hertzmark
What did she mean?

Ruby
>I don't know!
>and Aunt Babs is a spiritualist . . .
>so she takes me to a spiritualist church . . .

A spiritualist meeting gathers as . . .

Babs
>Mr Wedgewood is
>a medium for the world of Spirit . . .
>and will be talking to them on our behalf

Ruby
>I won't be spoken to
>because I don't know anybody who's dead . . .

Twins
>She doesn't remember.

Ruby
>and the dead talk to everybody
>through Mr Wedgewood

Wedgewood
>Spirit
>come and talk to us.

Ruby
>and the dead pop up all
>over the place . . .
>a woman's husband who's
>been dead for twenty years tells her

Wedgewood
>there's a light at the end of the tunnel . . .

Ruby
>there's the father of another woman
>who passed into Spirit last year who
>reports

Wedgewood
>he's missing the cinema . . .

Ruby
>somebody's mother comes back
>to tell her how to get rid of that
>scratch in her coffee table . . .

Wedgewood
>try linseed oil . . .

Ruby
>I'm beginning to droop . . . it's hot . . .
>when . . . he comes and stands in front
>of me . . .
>
>perhaps he knows I was only pretending
>to sing the hymn . . .
>
>but he says

Wedgewood
>your sister says not to worry about her

Ruby
>and that frightens me
>Auntie Babs . . .
>is Patricia . . . ?
>is Gillian . . .
>dead?

Babs
>Don't try to be clever, Ruby . . .
>it doesn't suit you . . .

Hertzmark
>What do you think she meant by that?

Ruby
>Maybe she thought I was being
>rude to Spiritualism!
>and then a visiting medium called

Myra who looks like Alma Cogan but
without the frocks . . .
gives a little talk on 'Animals
in the Spirit World' . . . which
poses the question . . . how
can there be enough room for everybody?

Stars twinkle and spin . . .

If all living things exist in the afterlife . . .
there must be zillion upon zillion of
plankton, amoeba, bacteria,
spinning off to the astral plane every day!
If not, then where do you draw the line?
Domestic pets?
Nothing smaller than a Yorkshire terrier?
A wasp?
And are they segregated . . . ?

Hertzmark
Ah . . . these cosmic questions . . .
being clever *does* suit you . . .

Ruby
And then . . .
I'm sitting on the carpet . . .
playing with Aunt Babs' ouija board thing
spelling the word
P
E
A
R
L
in a horseshoe shape

Ruby
I've learned to spell!
R–U–B–Y spells Ruby!
My name is Ruby.

I am a precious jewel.
I am a drop of blood.
I am Ruby Lennox.

but P–E–A–R– L . . . ?

Babs comes in, with Twins, sees the letters, picks them up, throws them in the fire . . . flare of red

Twins
She doesn't remember.

A fire flares and crackles . . .

Ruby
And then suddenly,
Teddy and I are free!
Back to *Home*!
Something has changed
Above The Shop

Bunty
Now, Ruby . . .

we've decided we're all going to
try and carry on and put the accident
behind us . . .

Hertzmark
Accident?

Ruby
I have no idea what she is talking
about . . .
no one appears to be hurt . . .
but . . . it's around then . . .
I begin walking in my sleep . . .

Music . . .

Ruby sleepwalks . . . explosions and sniper fire. She wanders through a World War One battlefield where . . .

NINE
JUST WALKING

Jack
I'm not going, Frank.

Frank
Not going where?

Jack laughs and points . . .

Jack
There . . . of course . . . No Man's Land.
I'm not going there.

Frank
Don't blame you, lad.

Jack
This new lieutenant's too nervous.
And mean.
I'm not going with him.
I went with the last one and he was
shot through the eye
dragging a wounded man back from . . . (*Points.*)
there
sniper got him
private helping him bought it as well
wounded lad died of gas gangrene anyway
so it was all for nothing . . .
done for me it did
that and the noise

Frank
Order comes to charge
I stumble
Jack turns to help me and . . .

Officer pokes a rifle in Jack's ribs . . .

Officer
Over the top, soldier.

Jack
Officer's generally lead from the front, sir.

You don't have to do that, sir
we're going

Half-drags Frank over top . . .

Run!

Frank runs, charging . . . Jack walks to . . . tell Nell, Lillian, listening . . .

Jack and **Ruby**
I just keep walking

Jack
I walk right across No Man's Land
mortars exploding around me
machine gun bullets
until . . . (*great surprise*)
I find myself right up against the barbed wire
fencing of the German trenches
find myself in a German trench!
I walk right along it till I come to
a dug-out
much better constructed than ours!
huddled in it
three German privates
one very blond
one very tall
one very stocky
(*amused*) I seen a music-hall act just like them
they'd danced and done a funny song
where they kept passing a top hat from
one head to another . . .
t'audience loved them . . .

but . . .
no one moves
so
in the end
I raise my Lee Enfield
fire off a clip

Gunfire . . .

each private flings his head back
then slides down the wall
last one has a look of surprise on his face . . .

Laughs.

and that wasn't a bad routine either!

I can't remember the song!

Lillian (*sings*)
The sun has got his hat on
hip hip hip hurray

Jack joins in, laughing . . . Nell watches . . .

the sun has got his hat on
and he's coming out to play . . .

Nell
I wish you'd wear your medal

Jack looks away from Nell, at Lillian . . .

A flapping of wings as . . .

TEN
INTERLUDE: 1950

Ruby
　　Bunty and the parrot went missing
　　on the same night . . .
　　it was only later
　　we realised it was just a coincidence
　　and they hadn't run away together . . .

　　A little dog yapping . . .

Patricia
　　Rags! Come on boy . . . Hup!

George
　　Where the bloody hell is she?

Patricia
　　Perhaps she left a note.

George
　　A note?

Patricia
　　Yes, a note.
　　You know, a note!

George
　　I know what a bloody note is!
　　I'm going to have that dog put down . . .

　　yapping and not selling all the
　　bloody time!

Ruby
　　Me and Patricia and Gillian
　　search the drawer in Bunty's
　　bedside table . . .
　　there's no note but . . .

What's this?

Alice's ghost, Nell's, attend as . . .

Gillian
It's a locket.
It's silver.

Ruby
Oh, it's me!

There are two tiny photographs
of me . . .
one in each wing of the locket

Patricia
This drawer *stinks* of Bunty's scent!

Ruby
Mummy's got a picture of me
by her bed . . .

Gillian
Oh yeah . . .
she's got that there because
it's a picture of P . . .

Patricia
Gillian!!!

Gillian
Ow!!!!
I'm telling Dad!

Patricia
Let's look in George's drawer . . .

Packet of Craven A

Gillian
Some money . . .
What's this?

Patricia
   Durex.
   God! . . . what a *Kid*!

Ruby
   Here's an envelope.

Patricia
   Open it.

Three (*reading*)
   'Dear George I have come
   to the end of my patience and feel I
   cannot go on in this vein much longer
   and I think it is better if I spend some
   time apart from you all.
   (*surprise as . . .*) Although you know how
   much I love the children . . .
   You say you are not running around with
   someone else and I must believe you as
   you are my husband but as you know
   life has not really been the same since P . . .'

Patricia
   Give me that!!!!!

   (*reads*) 'Well, anyway, I am going
   away for a bit because really I've
   had enough. Don't worry about me.
   As if you would, Bunty.'

   Best take this to George.
   Seal it up.

George
   You haven't opened this have you?

Patricia
   Of course we haven't.
   The envelope's sealed, isn't it?

George
> Well, anyway . . .
> your mother's had to go away
> suddenly to look after your Aunt
> Babs because she's feeling poorly.
> Auntie Babs that is.
> Feeling poorly.
> Not your mother.

Three
> Poor Auntie Babs . . .

Patricia
> So who's going to take us to
> Whitby for our holiday . . . ?

Hertzmark
> Who took you?
> For your holiday?

Ruby
> Auntie Doreen.

Hertzmark
> Who?

Ruby
> Auntie Doreen.
> A total stranger.

Hertzmark
> Was she frightening?

Lyrical happy music . . .

Ruby
> She was paradise
>
> kind   smiley   easy-going . . .
>
> she liked us all!

Doreen (*soft Belfast accent*)
You
must be Patricia because you're
the tallest . . .
and you must be Gillian because
you're the best dancer . . .
and you must be . . .

Ruby
Ruby.

Doreen
Ruby.
Because you're a precious jewel.

Ruby
We went to Whitby . . .

Seagulls . . . wind . . .

Patricia
This is where Dracula's ship
landed in a wild unnatural storm . . .
with all the crew dead
and those cliffs must be
where he ran up . . .
disguised as a black dog . . .
a hound of hell . . .

Doreen
My my
what a glorious imagination you have
Patricia . . .
Now shall we all have some
fish and chips?

Ruby
There's
order   and
. . . harmony in everything . . .

Doreen
> So this is where we're staying!
> What a lovely flat!
> Won't it be fun?
> And we can take turns *washing up
> and cleaning!* (*high treats*)

Ruby
> *I'll* wash up, Auntie Doreen!

Patricia
> *I'll* dry, Auntie Doreen!

Gillian
> Let *me* use the carpet-sweeper!

Ruby
> As calm and unflappable as a
> harbour-wall against the high
> tides of our emotions . . .

Three
> There's a *Beach*!

Patricia
> We have to make *Sandcastles*!
> But *I* say how many turrets!

Gillian
> I have to have some Rock!
> And some Candy Floss!
> And some Cinder Toffeeeee!

Ruby
> Can we go on the donkeys?
> Can we go in the sea?
> Can we bury each other on
> the sand and pretend we're dead?

Three
> We're hungry!

Can we have . . .
Fish and Chips Again?

Doreen
Of course we can . . .
we are on *Holiday* after all!

Gillian
Patricia's fallen off the Prom!

Three
She's sprained her wrist!

Ruby
But Auntie Doreen expertly
bandages and slings it . . .

Doreen
I was a nurse in the war . . .

Patricia
Ow!   Argh!   Eeech!

Doreen
Does it hurt?
I am sorry . . .
What a brave girl, Patricia, so you are . . .

Ruby
The contrast with Bunty is unavoidable

Patricia
Where do you come from, Auntie
Doreen?

Doreen
Why, Belfast, Patricia, Belfast.

Ruby
Where's that?

Gillian
> It's the capital of Wales!

Ruby
> We play Draughts Ludo
> Snakes and Ladders, Buccaneer
> but our favourite game is . . .

Three
> *Astron!*
>
> *Dauntless space music . . .*

Ruby
> Our spaceships have to move
> across the board scrolled across
> outer space dodging showers
> of meteorites
> asteroid belts
> rogue comets
> and before we achieve our goal . . .

Three
> *The Heart Of The Sun!!!*

Ruby
> We have to negotiate one
> last awful menace . . .

Three
> *The huge gaseous Rings of Saturn!!!*

Ruby
> The Rings of Saturn are *Deadly* . . .
> we know this because it says so
> on the Astron board
> and they're always catching
> Auntie Doreen's spaceship out . . .
>
> *Spaceship totalling sound as . . .*

Doreen
   Oh, there I go again!

Ruby
   She screams . . .
   as she explodes in a cloud of dust . . .

Ruby
   Even my sleepwalking seemed
   to stop with Auntie Doreen . . .

Hertzmark
   Who was she?
   This wonderful Auntie Doreen?

Ruby
   Something to do with George . . .
   she mentions Bunty a lot . . .

Doreen
   I'm sure Mummy wouldn't want
   you to do that, Gillian . . .

Ruby
   and . . .

Doreen
   I expect your Mummy's missing
   you, Patricia . . .

Ruby
   But when we ask if she
   actually knows Bunty, she
   laughs and splutters on her cigarette . . .

Doreen
   Goodness me, no!

Ruby
   George comes to collect us at
   the end of the week . . .

George
   Had a good time?
   I'll just sleep on the settee . . .

Ruby
   I wake early.
   I go down to the lounge for
   a last look at the sea . . .
   blue and sparkling as a sapphire . . .
   the settee's empty . . .
   George comes in . . . then Auntie
   Doreen . . .

   This happens as . . .

   She puts her arms round
   his waist from behind . . . her hands
   meet somewhere under his vest . . .

George
   Oungh! . . .

   God Doreen . . .

Ruby
   There's a look on his face
   I've never seen before . . .

Hertzmark
   What is it?

Ruby
   He was happy.

   Auntie Doreen
   do you have any children of your own?

Doreen
   No, dear . . .
   I had a little girl,
   but I lost her . . .

Patricia
   What was she called?

Doreen
   I don't know . . .

Ruby
   We drop Auntie Doreen in Leeds

Doreen
   Goodbye, me darlings!

Four
   Goodbye Auntie Doreen!

Ruby
   and we all go

All (*down*)
   Home to The Shop . . .

   Shop materialises as . . .

Ruby
   and . . . it's open!

Patricia
   Who's looking after The Shop?

George
   I closed up for the day . . . !

   Shop dings, a flurry of pet noises . . .

All
   Shop!

Bunty
   Oh, you're back then.

Gillian
   Mummy!

Patricia
Rags!

Ecstatic reunion . . . Patricia and Rags . . .

George
Bunty.

You're back!

Well . . . I'll put the kettle on, shall I?

Bunty
I'll do it.

George (*furtive fervent whisper*)
Listen!

You weren't on holiday with Auntie Doreen . . . do you understand?

Gillian and **Ruby**
Yes (*They're lying.*)

Patricia
Who *were* we on holiday with?

Who?

Who, Daddy, Who?

Bunty
Who looked after the shop all week?
It was closed when I got back.

George
When was that?

Bunty
About half an hour ago.

George
Walter's mother!

Bunty
We're low on cuttlefish.

George (*whisper*)
You Three!
I was with you in Whitby.
I was looking after you all week, right?

Girls
Right.

George
Remember, no Auntie Doreen.

Mum's the word.

Patricia
Daddy . . .
Can I keep Rags?
For my very own?

George
That's Blackmail!

Patricia
For my very own . . . ?

George
Yes, Buggar It!

Bunty
Let's have a Treat for tea!

Rest
Oh good! What?

Bunty (*beaming*)
Fish and chips of course!

Ruby
I'm woken in the pitch-black
of the night by something
scrabbling at the window!

Terrifying scrabbling . . .

Is it a ravenous vampire?

Is it Dracula?

It's not a vampire at all . . .

Tragic Parrot complaining . . .

It's the Parrot
it has the same expression of defeat
as George . . .
The holiday takes on the quality
of myth . . .
for a while we talked about
Auntie Doreen between ourselves . . .

Ruby
But by and by she became
as unreal as Mary Poppins . . .

Gillian
I saw Auntie Doreen skimming
along the West Pier . . .
didn't I? . . .
and then she circled those
green and red lights
by the harbour mouth . . .
didn't she?

Ruby
We never had the heart
to disenchant her . . .

Ruby and **Patricia**
Yes, Gillian . . .

Patricia
Now, Shut Up!

ELEVEN
AIRE AND ANGELS

At the front, Jack cleaning his rifle . . . Frank writing a letter . . .

Jack
Going back seems mad!

He laughs.

Frank
Why?

Jack
Marry Nell!
Become a father!
Dig an allotment!
Take me sons to a football match!

I can't see it . . .

Frank
Why not?

Jack
I think about
I think about . . .

Be no life with Nell . . .
too soft   and quiet   and gentle . . .

Lillian now . . .
bit more life about her . . .
eyes like a cat . . .
like she's secretly laughing at everything . . .

like everything's nonsense . . .

but most of all
I think about . . .

Albert appears . . .

a hot day a long time ago
swimming in the Ouse
me and Albert
Albert flopped on his belly
glistening with water like a fish . . .

Albert
Frank and I taught each other to
swim here
just at this spot . . .

Jack sits up, looks at the skin on Albert's back . . .

Jack
His skin's more beautiful than any woman's

Albert laughs, his face buried in his arms.

What's funny?

his shoulder blades quivering . . .

He reaches out, touches Albert's shoulder . . .

You can easily imagine
any minute
the little nubs of wings would
push through the satin skin over his
shoulder . . .

I have to stop myself . . .

What's funny?

Albert gets up, runs off, dives in . . .

Don't know what made him laugh.

Maybe just happiness.

Albert shouts from a long way off . . .

Albert
   We had a right good day, didn't we?

Jack
   He had an extraordinary capacity for
   happiness, Albert . . .

Albert
   A right good day!

Nell
   Albert collected good days the way
   other people collect coins
   or sets of postcards.

   She joins the next scene as . . .

TWELVE
SNOW FEATHERS: 1959

Christmas music . . .

Crystal snow tingling . . .

George (*calling up*)
   Ruby!

   Ruby!

   Ruby!!!

Ruby
   What?
   I'm curled up on my pink
   candlewick bedspread with an old
   copy of Gillian's *Judy* . . . I have to share
   with Gillian now because Grandma's
   moved in with us because

George
>She's not the full shilling . . .

Nell
>Where am I?
>Is this the War?
>Am I married?
>Who to?
>Mother?

George
>Ruby!
>Your mother could do with some help!

Nell picks up a piece of tinsel . . .

Bunty
>Do you know what time it is?
>Where have you been?

Silence.

>With your Floozy I suppose?

George
>Don't be ridiculous!
>I've been having a pint in
>The Punch Bowl with Walter.

Bunty
>I can't imagine what she sees in you.
>It can't be your looks?
>And it's certainly not your money!
>What do you do . . . pay her?

George (*mildly*)
>Have you seen the
>Evening Press anywhere . . .?

Nell ties a piece of tinsel round her neck.

Ruby
We are going to the pantomime
tonight, aren't we?

Bunty
Why else do you think I'm going
flat out like this?
And I haven't time to make a pudding.
It'll have to be tinned fruit.
Haven't you got anything to do, Ruby?

Ruby
I haven't.
I didn't think you needed to have
anything to do on Christmas Eve

Nell
I should be sewing them uniforms! . . .
but I'm so . . .

Nell sits down in a chair, falls asleep.

George
Where's our Gillian?

Bunty
Piano lesson.

Ruby
Gillian bursts into the room . . .

She throws her music case down and sprawls in a chair revealing her navy-blue knickers.

She sighs darkly
crossing her legs

Gillian sighs darkly . . . for a ten-year-old.

Bunty
You're not supposed to cross your legs.

Ruby
> Listen Gillian . . .
> this is your last day on earth . . .
> lighten up for heaven's sake . . .

George
> Tea's ready

Ruby
> Patricia wanders in . . .
> reading . . .

George
> You took your time

Patricia
> Yes, yes, I did take a long time,
> didn't I . . .?

Ruby
> He wants to hit her but she's
> accidently met the Floozy . . .

Bunty (*singing*)
> Take me back to the Black Hills
> the Black Hills of Dakota . . .
> to the beautiful Indian country
> that I love . . .

George
> Pork's a bit tough.

Bunty
> Really?
> Really?
> Really?
>
> What a wet night for going out!

Gillian
>Can I sit next to you at the pantomime,
>Daddy?

George
>Of course, pet.

Bunty
>If you don't hurry up, Ruby . . .
>you'll be sitting here when *we're*
>all at the pantomime!

Ruby
>She says this as if she's pleased
>with herself for saying something
>clever.
>Is this my real mother?
>Why does she do this?

George
>Yes, stop dithering, Ruby, you
>can't spend your whole life being
>late, you know . . . !

Ruby
>I start to eat as fast as I can . . .
>
>As soon as she can . . .
>Bunty whisks the plates away . . .
>I think she would prefer it if
>she could wash up before we'd eaten . . .
>
>she waltzes back with the cutglass bowl
>containing tinned sliced peaches

Bunty
>that are like big smiles . . .
>like the enormous manic smile
>fixed on her own face . . .

Patricia
I don't want any!

Bunty
That's too bad.
I need the bowl for Boxing Day
trifle . . .

Patricia
Well, alright . . .
They say discretion is the better part of
valour, don't they, Father?

Ruby
George has no idea what she's talking
about, but he's pretty sure it's
something to do with The Floozy . . .

George
Pass the cream . . .

Ruby
He cuts a peach slice . . .
scoops a little cream on it . . .
raises it delicately to his lips . . .

George
The cream's off.

Ruby
He stares at Bunty,
daring her to contradict him

Patricia (*tastes it*)
Off.

Ruby
All thought of festive goodwill
has been abandoned.

Bunty licks her lips with the
fastidiousness of a cat . . .

Bunty
Tastes alright to me.

Ruby
She's being very brave,
rather like Deborah Kerr in
The King and I . . .

George
You bloody eat it then!

Ruby
Which leaves Gillian in a bit of a dilemma
her cheeks stuffed with rancid cream
and slippery peaches . . .
not sure which parent to suck up to . . .

Gillian . . . mouthful of rancid food . . . as . . .

Ruby
and then the happy family
is off to The Pantomime!

Bunty
We're off then, Mother!

Nell (*waking*)
Is it an air raid?
Is it Teatime?

Ruby (*dread*)
And we're at the Theatre Royal
watching The Pantomime!

Roar of children's audience screaming . . .

Gillian
She's behind you!
She's behind you!!!!

Hertzmark
>The witch, an elf, a panda, a cow
>and a plucky village youth rush
>about the stage while Hansel and
>Gretel hide under some leaves . . .

Patricia
>The panda's winning . . .

Gillian
>They want a volunteer from the
>audience . . . !
>Me!
>Choose ME!
>ME!!!!!

Bunty
>Well, really . . .
>She is a one, our Gillian . . .

Ruby
>She does a very spirited . . .

Gillian (*sings*)
>On the good ship, lollipop . . .
>it's a short walk
>to the candy-shop . . .

Ruby
>and then . . .

Bunty
>All good things come to an end.

George
>Well, that's over for another year!

Hertzmark
>the witch is burned to a heap
>of charred rags . . .
>the wicked stepmother's pardoned . . .

children reclaimed . . .
Hansel and Gretel find the witch's
treasures overflowing with emeralds
diamonds opals

Ruby
Rubies . . .
glowing like the bag of boiled sweets
Gillian and I are sharing . . .
The Good Fairy sends a shower of
glitter from her wand so thick that
when I put out my hand
I can touch it . . .

Gillian (*bursting into tears*)
Oh no . . .
It's Over!!!!

Bunty (*to strangers*)
Sorry . . . she's very tired . . .
children you know . . .
(*to Gillian*) Why don't you just
bloody grow up, Gillian?

Ruby
It's unfortunate for Bunty
that these are her last words to Gillian . . .
the one thing Gillian is clearly *not*
going to do is grow up . . .
(*to Gillian*) Do you want the last red one . . .
or can I have it?

Gillian
I'll have it.

Traffic . . . crowd . . . outdoors . . .

Ruby
We're outside the Theatre Royal.

George is hopping around trying
to catch a taxi . . .

George
Taxi! You . . . Damn!

Ruby
The rain is turning to needles of sleet . . .

Patricia
I'm not standing with *You Lot*!
I don't want anybody who *knows*
me to see me with *You Lot*!

Ruby
Bunty, for some reason, is
holding tightly onto my hand as
we shiver on the pavement . . .

Bunty
Stand *Still*!

Ruby
She's making a big mistake . . .
she's holding on to the wrong child
because . . .

Gillian (*delight*)
Look! My friends from *school*!
They've seen me!
Hello! Hello!

Bunty
Don't . . .

Ruby
I don't see what happens next . . .
but I suppose Gillian has run out from
between the parked cars
without looking

Busy cars, traffic noise . . . talking, shouting . . .

because all of a sudden
there is a bang
and a pale blue Hillman Husky van
is lobbing her gently into the path
of the taxi George has succeeeded
in hailing . . .

It's not much of a Christmas.

George and Bunty . . . vanish.
It's just me
and Patricia
and Grandma
and the Pets.

Nell
I can't cope.

Patricia
There's a Christmas stocking.

Ruby
I know.

My stocking for Christmas 1959
contains (in reverse order from the
toe upwards) a sixpence, a walnut,
an orange, a pack of Happy Family
playing cards, a bar of Fry's
Peppermint Cream and a cheap,
rather pink, doll wearing a knitted
vest and knickers.

Patricia
Disgusting.

Ruby
I've had better.

We make an effort.
I switch on the Christmas tree lights.

Nell
Is it Christmas?

Patricia
I'll clean out the grate
and lay out a new fire, I suppose . . .

Ruby
We look doubtfully
at the pile of presents under the tree . . .

Patricia
May as well open them . . .

Ruby
She shrugs her shoulders in that way
she has of suggesting she couldn't care
less about anything . . .
although, of course, she cares terribly.
About everything.

I've got a white fur muff.

Patricia
Open that.

Ruby
The Railway Children . . .

Patricia
That's from me.
Alright?

Ruby
From beyond the grave,
Gillian has sent me . . .

Opens it . . . it is a brown bri-nylon dog with a purple ribbon round its fat neck, holding a green and purple bottle of April Violets cologne . . .

Patricia
That's disgusting.

Ruby
Disgusting.

I think Patricia and I should
share Gillian's presents but I know
this isn't the right attitude

Patricia
Merry Christmas, Ruby.

Ruby
Merry Christmas, Patricia.

She doesn't try to cook the turkey . . .
For Christmas dinner we have

Patricia
mashed potatoes
baked beans
and corned beef . . .

Nell
I can't cope.

Ruby
Although only after we've both lacerated
ourselves opening the corned-beef tin . . .

Patricia and **Ruby**
Owwwwh!

Nell
Lillian!

Ruby
>And then snow starts falling . . .
>great flakes like goose feathers . . .
>
>*Sound of geese . . .*
>
>and I start spinning the glass balls
>on the Christmas tree . . .
>
>*Very distressed . . .*
>
>if I can work hard at it . . .
>I can get them all spinning at
>the same time . . .
>
>That's enough for now.

Hertzmark
>Little break, Ruby . . .
>
>*She opens a drawer somewhere . . . gets out a steaming cup of tea and a hot mince pie . . . hands it to Ruby . . . then to us, the audience . . .*
>
>Little break for you too . . .
>cup of tea . . .
>. . . coffee . . . alcoholic beverages . . .
>Little visit to the toilet . . . ?
>
>That would be my prognosis . . .
>
>*She smiles as . . .*
>
>*Music . . .*
>
>*Light fades . . .*
>
>*It is the . . .*
>
>*Interval.*

Act Two

THIRTEEN
THE DOGS OF WAR

World War One . . . music . . . lingering smoke . . .

A little girl is seen, then gone . . .

Everybody (*praying*)
Dear God . . .
I do not ask that I do not die
I know that's not an option . . .

Frank
It's been two years and the odds against me
are piled high
I just ask that you let me see it coming
let me see the mortar coming
so I can prepare myself
let me anticipate in some magical way
the sniper's bullet that's going to take
my brain out
before my body knows about it . . .
please please don't let me be
gassed
and please look after Jack even though he
has betrayed me and got a job with . . .

A lot of yipping and yelping . . .

Jack
Dogs!

Jack walks on, accompanied by a very intelligent, adoring, obedient . . .

Frank
You jammy bugger!

. . . Jack Russell terrier . . . called . . .

Jack
Pep!
Sit!
Lie!
Die for England.

Frank
The kennels are back from the Front a ways . . .

Jack
Pep

Jack and **Nell**
is the fastest and best messenger dog of all

He demonstrates. Takes out a piece of paper. Reads it.

Jack
'More ammo needed in South-forward trench'

Folds it up, attaches it to Pep's collar

People give their family pets for the War Effort.

He holds Pep, quoting . . .

'We have let Daddy go and fight the
Kaiser . . .
now we are sending Pep to do his bit.
love . . . Flora.'

Frank
You'd be more worried if a sniper
got that bloody dog than me . . .

Jack
Good dog, Pep.

He takes out . . .

Nell
Rabbit's foot.
For luck

Gives it to Pep.

Pep!

Another space . . . Patricia, with Rags . . .

Patricia
Rags!

Both
Sit!

Jack
and . . .
March!

Both march off . . . Patricia stays training Rags as . . .

FOURTEEN
FIRE! FIRE! 1960

Hertzmark (*reading*)
'Gillian Berenice Lennox
14th January 1948 to 24th December 1959
Beloved Daughter of George and Bunty.
Safe in the arms of Jesus'

Hmm.

How are things at home after that?

Ruby?

Ruby
Everybody's busy!

Bunty
I've piles of ironing to do!
Piles!

This place is bloody freezing!

George
We've run out of paraffin, that's why!
Just slipping out!
I won't be long!

Bunty
Very likely!

George
I'm just slipping out then!

Patricia
I'm reading volume three
of *A la recherhe du temps perdu*
it's about the metaphysical ambiguity
of reality, time, and death and the power
of sensation to retrieve
memories and reverse time . . .

Nell (*to Bunty*)
Here
My mother's locket.

She gives her the locket again . . .

Nell
I meant to give it to Babs when I died . . .
but your spirits seem so low
considering you're getting married tomorrow . . .

Bunty
You've already given me it, Mother!
And I'm married already.
So bloody married!

She takes it anyway . . .

Ruby
Everything's suddenly Dangerous!

Bunty
Be careful of that knife!
You'll poke your eye out with that pencil!
Hold onto the banister!
Watch that umbrella!

Ruby
I mind the shop . . .

Pet sounds . . .

I sell two kittens . . . one tortoise-shell
one ginger
a very winsome puppy
two gerbils
a hamster wheel three bags of sawdust
six pounds of biscuit mix a dog basket
one gemstone cat collar (diamonds, fake)
and an enormous Belgian rabbit
Daddy . . . I've just sold a rab . . .

George
Where's your mother?

Ruby
Did you get the paraffin?

George
I forgot the bloody paraffin!

How can I go and get paraffin
if your mother's not here?

Ruby
I can manage.

George
    No you can't.

    Go and get Patricia . . . she can mind the shop . . .

Ruby
    My heart sinks . . .
    getting Patricia is invariably my job
    and it's a thankless task . . .
    I climb upstairs slowly . . .
    I pass Bunty's bedroom . . .

    she's looking in her dressing-room mirror . . .

Bunty
    My Gillian
    my pearl . . .

    Oh!

    Oh, it's only you.

Ruby
    It's just me.
    Just Ruby!

    She hammers on Patricia's door . . .

Patricia
    Go away!

Ruby
    Daddy wants you.

Patricia
    Go away.
    Tell him I'm ill.

Ruby
    What shall I say's wrong with you?

Patricia (*Proustian*)
　I have sickness of the soul.

Ruby
　Shall I tell Daddy that?
　'Patricia can't come down, her soul's
　sick'?

Patricia
　Tell him I've got my period –
　that'll shut him up!

Ruby
　She's right, it does.

George
　Typical.
　Well, I'm going out anyway.

Ruby
　I'm glad to say all the pets
　receive a lot of attention from me
　on that fateful day . . .
　I fluff the kittens up
　let the hamsters run along the counter
　I play *Grrrr* with Rags . . .
　I even try to talk to the Parrot

　Pretty Polly!

　Who's a pretty parrot?

Ruby
　George comes back with a
　lot of paraffin . . .

Bunty
　Mind that paraffin heater!

Ruby
　then . . .

George
>I'm just slipping out!

Ruby
>It's a quiet domestic evening.

Bunty
>Tea's ready!
>Get Patricia.

Ruby
>She's not very well.
>It's her soul.

Bunty
>Just get her, Ruby, don't be
>clever!

Hertzmark
>They really don't want you to
>be clever, do they?

Ruby
>We have sausages for tea.
>
>I play Scrabble with myself.
>I go to bed . . .
>nobody checks I've brushed my teeth . . .
>nobody even checks I've gone
>to bed at all . . .
>I pray for Gillian to be very happy
>in Heaven and not be upset
>about being dead . . .
>meanwhile, downstairs . . .
>
>Bunty is ironing . . .
>she discovers . . .

Bunty
>Gillian's pink viyella blouse
>amongst the pile . . . (*Runs out.*)

Patricia
  Actually, it's only my Sunday
  knickers . . .

Ruby
  Above The Shop smells of sausages . . .

  Both Patricia and Ruby gag . . .

Hertzmark
  Something happens . . .?

Ruby and **Ghosts**
  The iron just keeps getting hotter
  and hotter . . . it's scorching the
  cheerful red gingham cloth of the
  ironing board . . .
  the pad underneath darkens . . .
  the flames find the wood frame
  the melting flex falls to the floor and
  finds the linoleum . . .
  one particular energetic flame goes
  whoosh!
  and stretches up and reaches
  the curtains!
  then there's no stopping it
  it gobbles up
  everything in its path . . .
  all the kitchen . . .
  wallpaper
  salt and pepperpots
  but it's not enough
  it leaves the kitchen
  popping its head out of the door
  and across the passage
  into the
  Shop where
  there are wonderful things to play with . . .

paraffin
sawdust
and the whispering, rustling noise of
fear . . .

Explosion . . .

Patricia
Ruby! Ruby!

Ruby
The end of the world!

Patricia
Get *up*, Ruby, Get out of bed!

Fire, Ruby, Fire!

I'm not sure we can go out there!

Patricia
Help me get the clothes off the bed . . .

Ruby
Why . . .?

Patricia
stuff them under the door . . .
stop the smoke . . .!
Here . . . we've got to wrap these
school blouses round our faces . . .

Ruby
we look like the Lone Ranger . . .

Lone Ranger music . . .

Patricia
Stand back!
I'm going to break the window!

Smash of glass . . .

It's alright . . . the fire brigade will
be here soon . . .

Breathe in!   Fresh Air!

Sound of Pet screams . . .

Ruby
What's that noise?

Patricia
Pets!
Someone's got to help the Pets!

Stay there, don't move!

I'm going down the drainpipe . . .
you stay there!

Stay there . . . help will be here soon!

I'll get the fire brigade!

Ruby
You could trust Patricia
in a way you never could Gillian . . .

I'm alone in a burning building . . .
but Patricia said stay there . . .
so I wait until I see a
fireman climbing slowly towards me . . .

Fireman
Hello, sweetheart
let's get you out of there
shall we?

Ruby
From my excellent bird's eye view
I can see the Back Yard is buzzing with life . . .

Together . . .

Patricia
Come on, Ruby! Come down!

Bunty (*screaming*)
Aaaaaagh! Aaaagh!

George
Shut up, Bunty! Just shut up!

Ruby
The incredible shrinking family . . .

I'm waiting for Bunty to say
something like *I told you to be
more careful!* but she says
nothing at all

*Bunty wraps Ruby in her dressing-gowned arms,
cries . . .*

Sound of Bunty crying . . .

Mummy . . . !

Ruby
The ghosts aren't the least bit surprised . . .

Hertzmark
No . . .
York has been scoured and destroyed
by fire many times . . .
the melted stained-glass panels . . .
blackened centurion's helmets . . .
frizzled periwigs . . .

Ruby
I've seen the reeking, charcoaled
insides of The Shop!
I've smelt the unforgettable smell
of toasted fur and feather . . .
no lime tisane and madeleines for us
in future years . . .
it was amazing what the
smell of frying sausage
could achieve . . .

Nell is still standing in the scene, sniffing the air . . .

Nell
Jack?
Jack?

Jack, with Pep . . .

Jack
Message . . .
front line trench . . .
they need more magazines for the Lewis Guns
Pep goes at his usual hop, skip and jump pace . . .
little stumpy tail making his whole body wag . . .
and

Burst of gun fire . . .

he's caught . . .
right at the top of a bounding arc . . .
he falls to the ground
back leg splintered by shrapnel . . .
horrible   yelping   noise
all the time he's trying to scrabble back
to his feet and carry on running . . .

Come on boy
come on lad . . .

He's too . . .

He's down, crawling out to the dog . . .

Frank
He's not reached Pep before . . .

Explosion . . .

Nell
a grenade rips him to pieces

Jack dies . . .

Frank
>Pep howls and howls for Jack

Frank
>until . . .

Nell
>A British sniper manages to hit
>the little dog . . .

Sniper's Voice (*off*)
>One more minute
>that howling!
>I'd put a bullet through me own brain!

Frank
>I got his rabbit foot
>Had no more trouble with death until 1942
>Came home
>Married Nell

Nell
>Small church wedding.
>I wore Lilac . . . Lillian

Lillian
>Grey.

Both
>Pearl-buttoned gloves
>big hats
>floating veils . . .

Frank
>They looked like Moths.
>I wish I could have married both of them
>
>Thought I saw Jack
>
>Thought I saw Albert

Thought for some reason they'd come for
Lillian

Lillian
I'm going to have a baby.

Nell
Oh, Lillian.

Frank
They'd come for Rachel.
She dropped down dead
just as we were about to
leave for our honeymoon
in the Lake District.

Rachel (*furious*)
I've been very disappointed
with life! (*She dies.*)

Nell
I never loved him. Frank.

Bunty
I loved Edmund.

Lillian
Edmund.

Ruby
After the Fire
just *one* miracle occurs . . .

Fireman
Does this little chap belong to
anyone . . . ?

Little dog yipping . . .

Patricia
Rags!
Oh Rags!

Hertzmark
>The sky is streaked with red as
Pets' blood streams
in the firmament.
Flocks of budgies turn into angels
with Technicolour wings
and wheel across the sky.

Ruby
>Perhaps in the Spirit World . . .
the Parrot will have been given
The Gift of Tongues . . .

Hertzmark
>and loved.
Many things are uncertain . . .

Ruby
>but one thing is sure . . .
this morning . . .
the arms of Jesus are
very full indeed.

Hertzmark
>The Great Fire of London *purged*
the Great Plague . . .

Ruby
>and the Great Pet Shop Fire

Ruby
>purges the death of Gillian . . .

Patricia
>If she'd been alive . . .
she'd have died in the fire . . .
so she'd be dead anyway . . .
Right?

Bunty
Our days above The Shop are *Over*!

George
I've been down the Leeds and Holbeck
building society
secured a nice little mortgage on . . .

Bunty
a nice little semi . . .

Both
no more PETS.

Bunty
A new line of business . . .

George
Medical and Surgical Supplies!
Trusses, wheelchairs, hearing-aids,
elastic stockings . . . there's no end to it!
There'll be stuff on prescription
from doctors . . .
walk-in trade for stuff like Elastoplasts
and Durex.

Bunty
Durex?
There'll be some brass in that!

Ruby (*whisper*)
Durex?
What's that?

Patricia
I'll tell you later.

Ruby
But she never did.

Music . . .

FIFTEEN
THE RINGS OF SATURN

Lights on Lillian somewhere, clearing out a box. Nell watching and nearby, a baby's cradle . . .

Lillian
Rachel's dead and buried.
Good riddance.
I'm chucking out.

Albert, Frank and Jack hover by baby, trying to see . . .

He's mine. Just mine.
I'm calling him Edmund.
I'm not saying who the father is.

Nell
Has he got black hair?

Lillian
He's got golden curls like an angel
and eyes the colour of forget-me-nots . . .
Here. Mother's locket.
You can have it.
Because you were just the baby . . .
she never even held you . . .

Lillian gives Nell the locket. Lights dim, rise on . . .

Ruby
The remaining female Lennoxes
are teetering between the two worlds
of innocence and experience . . .
for me this is symbolised by the
Eleven Plus . . .
for Patricia . . .

Patricia
I'm about to lose my virginity!!!

Ruby
Do you want me to help you find it?

Patricia
Don't be so clever . . .
Can I talk to you, or are you
just being stupid?

Ruby
She's being courted by Howard
an earnest bespectacled twig of a boy
from St Peter's . . .

Patricia
I've decided to do it with him

Bunty (*off*)
Patricia!

Patricia
Howard's parents are going away
next weekend so we'll do it then . . .
look what I've got . . .
'Chubby Checker's Dancin' Party'

Ruby
Are you in love with Howard,
Patricia?

Patricia (*snorts*)
Come off it, Ruby!
Romantic Love's an outmoded
convention!
Let me get to the Dansette . . .

Bunty
Patricia!

Patricia
But it is nice to have someone who
wants you, you know?
(*to Bunty*) Whaaaaaaaat?

Chubby Checker's Dancin' Party starts up . . .

Ruby
Bunty's very suspicious . . .

Ruby and **Patricia** (*singing*)
Let's twist again . . .
Like we did last summer . . .
C'mon let's twist again
Like we did last year . . .

Bunty
If I thought for just one moment
you'd been . . .

Patricia
Enjoying myself?

Ruby
Her supercilious expression
is just asking to be erased by a slap.
But no slap.

Bunty starts to quiver . . .

Patricia
Is something wrong . . . Mummy?

Bunty
Wrong?
Only you – that's the only thing
that's wrong with me!

Patricia
What a bloody cow you are!

Ruby
  . . . it's only at dinner . . .
when she's dishing up the butter
beans that look like pale little
foetuses curling up on the 'Harvest'

Bunty crying as . . .

dinner plates that Bunty finally
dissolves . . .

The first part of the Eleven Plus
seems suspiciously easy

'Write about one of the following:
(a) A busy street scene
(b) A visit to the swimming
baths
(c) What would you do if you had Aladdin's
lamp for the day

(*voice-over*) And I chose Aladdin's lamp . . .
long a favourite daydream . . .
and am lulled into thinking
that everything is going to be alright . . .

two weeks later I sit the arithmetic
paper and I'm reeling
with horror as I leave School
How many stamps ½ in. by ¾ in.
will cover a sheet of paper 6 in. by
8 in.?

A grocer mixes 4 pounds of tea
3s 6d per pound. He sells the
mixture
5s per pound.
What is his profit?

Who am I to know the answer to
these questions?

Patricia
How was it?

Ruby can't speak . . .

Let's walk along the Ouse . . .

Ruby
This is the coldest winter since 1947
I've never seen a river frozen like this.

Patricia
It used to freeze nearly every winter
in the olden days . . .
Did you know that?

Ruby
Of course I didn't know that.
I know nothing.

As we stand watching
the frozen river . . .
a curious feeling rises up inside me
a feeling of something long forgotten . . .
it has something to do with

cold

and . . . the ice
and something to do with water too . . .

I try to concentrate on the feeling
bring it to life
but as soon as I do

it evaporates

It's like when I wake from
sleepwalking . . .

and I know I've lost something
incredibly important . . .
something that's been torn out of me
leaving a hole inside . . .

Patricia
Are you alright, Ruby?

Ruby
but we're diverted by
the approach of two swans,
balanced forlornly on their own
private iceberg . . .

This is created . . .

We can hear the river cracking.

And crackling.

What are you doing here anyway?

Patricia
Truanting.
Do you think those swans are
alright?

Ruby
Well . . . I would change places
with them anytime . . .
at least the rest of their lives
doesn't depend on whether
they can do mental arithmetic . . .

Patricia
And they can fly away if they
want to

Ruby
And they have each other.

The water looks so cold.

Patricia
   It is.
   . . . Ruby?

Ruby
   What?

Patricia
   Do you remember . . .

Hertzmark
   Ask her!

Patricia
   Nothing. It doesn't matter.
   . . . Come on . . . I'll wait with you
   at the bus-stop if you like . . .

Ruby
   And she turned her collar
   up against the wind

Hertzmark
   . . . she knew something you didn't . . .

Ruby
   Yes.

Hertzmark
   But you haven't asked her?

Ruby
   No.

   She starts exhibiting an unusual buoyancy . . .

Patricia
   I'm enjoying discovering
   the Bohemian joys of sex with Howard . . .

Ruby
   This new hobby causes her to forget
   to revise for her mock O-levels

and she fails them all dismally . . .
Her favourite things now are . . .

Patricia
Howard
The Campaign For Nuclear Disarmament
The Beatles . . . the Fab Four . . . !

Ruby
Her least favourite thing is . . .

Patricia
Bunty!
You Lot!

Bunty
You're not my child!

Patricia
Thank God!

Ruby
And Bunty locks her out of
the house, so she's unable
to creep in as usual at three o'clock
in the morning . . .

Patricia (*drunken shouting . . .*)
Bloody bourgeois
pigs . . . come the revolution . . .
you'll be first against the wall,
Bunty Lennox!

Ruby
It creates quite a stir in the
dark neighbourhood . . .

Voice
Shut up!
Folk are trying to sleep!

Ruby
> I think Patricia's quite enjoying
> herself and almost looks
> annoyed when I throw my
> front-door key down to her . . .

She has an almost empty bottle of Bristol Cream Sherry . . . from which she takes an occasional slug . . .

Patricia
> I've fallen out with Howard . . .
>
> He's decided he's going to be
> an accountant . . .

She struggles to light a cigarette, an expression of disgust on her face . . .

Ruby
> And what are you going to be,
> Patricia?

Patricia
> Dunno.

She blows out a stream of thoughtful smoke and knocks ash everywhere . . .

> I think I'd just like to be happy.

Ruby
> Well, if I had Aladdin's lamp
> for the day, Patricia, that's
> exactly what you would be.

Bunty
> Shift yourself, Ruby!

Ruby
> Our new neighbours are . . .
> the Ropers . . .

Ropers appear as a unit . . . Mr, Mrs, with Christine, Kenneth and screaming baby David . . .

Roper
Well, hel-*lo* there!

Instant lust between Bunty and Roper . . . they lose no opportunity to have their hands on one another throughout this next section . . .

Bunty
He's an *ex-squadron leader*!!!

Mrs Roper
Christine . . .

Christine
Lo.

Mrs Roper
Kenneth . . .

Kenneth
Lo.

Mrs Roper
. . . baby David . . .
baby David make a teapot . . .

Mrs Roper is in love with baby David, who leaks a lot . . .

Ruby
It isn't long before I'm playing ball with Rags and . . .

Rags! Rags!
Fetch! . . .
Tut . . .

Fetching the ball, she comes across Bunty and Mr Roper fucking . . .

Oh!

There's something nasty poking out from
Mr Roper's cavalry twill . . .

Roper
Well, hel'*lo*!

Ruby backs out . . .

Ruby
and then . . .

George
I've been having a chat with Clive Roper . . .

Bunty (*innocent*)
Oh?

George
What d'you think about going on holiday
with the Ropers this summer?

Bunty (*joy unconfined*)
The Ropers?

Ruby and **Patricia** (*horror unconfined*)
The Ropers?

Immediately . . .

Ruby
The Hammer Holiday from Hell is about to begin!

All
We're off!

*A lightning journey through Scotland . . . two cars . . .
the Roper car and the Lennox car . . .*

Patricia
Why are we following him?

Bunty
He's the only one who knows how to
get to Scotland . . .

he's overtaking someone! . . . Quick, quick . . . put your indicator on!

George
What the bloody hell is he doing?
There's that bloody fish and chip shop again!

Patricia
Where's Rags?
Who's looking after Rags?
What about Rags?

Bunty
Be Quiet in The Back!

Nell
This *is* the Lake District!
Oh *Noooo*! . . . I'm on my Honeymoon!!!!

Mrs Roper
Did you see what she's wearing?
So low-cut for Scotland!

Kenneth
I'm bored.

Christine
My tummy's sore.

Bunty
B125 . . . B126 . . . What's the difference?

George
I knew we should have come by Newcastle.

Patricia
When are we going to eat?

Bunty
Eat?

Patricia
   Yes, eat, you know . . . eat, food, ever heard of it?

George
   Don't talk to your mother like that!

Nell
   If it's me honeymoon . . .
   he's going to make me have sex!!!!

Mrs Roper
   She's bursting out of that blouse!

Kenneth
   I'm bored!

Christine
   My tummy's sore

Bunty
   He's slowing down! He's stopping!

Roper
   Grub Stop!

Mrs Roper
   Baby David make a teapot!

Patricia
   Nothing for me thanks!

All
   This doesn't look very appetising!

   Nell eats regardless . . .

Roper
   Chocks Away!

   Baby David is sick . . . Mrs Roper holds him out the window . . .

Bunty
What's wrong with you, Patricia?

Ruby
Is it your soul, Patricia?

All
Shutupruby.

Ruby
as we descend into Oban,
we can see . . .

All
The Sea!

Bunty
Keep yourself occupied, can't you?

Ruby
Let's play Spot the . . .

Spot . . . a red car . . .

All
There!

There!

Patricia
Spot . . . a handsome man . . .

Bunty
Mr Roper!

Ruby
Spot . . . someone wearing a kilt!

There is no one wearing a kilt . . .

Mrs Roper
and she's going to twist an ankle
walking in heather in those shoes!

Kenneth
  I'm bored!

Christine (*rubbing tummy*)
  Oooh . . . aergh . . .

Bunty
  How should *I* know what the sign said?
  You're the Driver!

Nell
  Lillian . . . you gave me mother's locket
  when I came back off my honeymoon . . .
  didn't you?

Patricia
  Yes, Grandma . . .

Bunty
  Sauchiehall Street . . .

Patricia
  Dunbarton . . .

Ruby
  Crianlarich

George
  How did he find Dresden?

Patricia
  Spot the rain.

All
  Rain   rain   rain . . .

Bunty
  What's he doing?
  He's turning he's turning!

Roper
  Pit stop!

All stop, pile out . . . Mrs Roper holds baby out to pee . . . everybody chilly . . .

Nell
Frank, can we go home now?

Roper
I wish you were in my car!

Bunty
I wish I was in your car!

All back in cars . . .

Bunty
Sheep!

Patricia
Spot the sheep

George
Does this road have a number?

I wish he'd put his bloody lights on!

Bunty
There's one!   Mind that one!
That one's going to cross!

All
We're Here!

Children
It's horrible!
It looks like *Colditz*!

Roper
Shall I carry that for you, Bunty?

Mrs Roper
George, could you carry that for me?

Nell
This food's shit!

Roper
What about a spot of sightseeing?

Kenneth
I'm bored!

Christine (*in pain*)
Oooooooh . . .

All
Fort William!

Patricia
Why's it famous?

Ruby
A massacre . . .

Patricia
Oh good!

Ruby
No . . . a *historical* one . . .

All
Rain

Roper
Bunty . . . have you seen this volcanic plug?

Mrs Roper
George . . . could you get me a new nappy out of the . . . Too Late!

Ruby
I'm cold!

Nell
I'm hungry!

Patricia
    I feel . . . (*She is sick.*)

Christine
    I feel . . . ooooo---ergh . . .

Kenneth
    I'm bored!

Roper
    This is The Bottomless Loch!
    Apparently . . . it's Bottomless!

Ruby
    Let's not go on it . . .

Bunty
    What about The Sea?

Roper
    A little boat trip, perhaps?
    Or should I see 'A wee boat trip' . . . hahaha . . .

Bunty finds his wit beyond wonderment . . .

Patricia (*reading*)
    Trips round the bay . . .
    Mr A. Stewart – Proprietor . . .

He appears . . . Hertzmark . . .

George
    Donald, where's your troosers, hoots mon!

Bunty
    Shut up, George!

Mrs Roper affects to find George very amusing . . .

They form into a small boat party . . .

Bunty
    Oh no.

Roper
What is it?

Sea gets choppier . . .

Bunty and Roper rubbing up against one another . . . surreptitiously . . .

Baby David a little teapot again . . .

Bunty heaves up . . .

Roper
Poor Bunty!

George
That's one and ninepence worth of
fish and chips!

Boatman
It's just a wee squall!

Roper
Wee or not . . .
I don't think this boat is up to
a squall old chap!

Christine (*dreadful pain*)
ergh . . . ogh . . . agh . . .

Huge storm blows up . . .

Ruby
The blue of the sea grows claret-dark
and
trouble brews
gusts of wind batter and buffet . . .
I shuffle up to Patricia
we hold hands   squeezing tight
we cling to each other in terror . . .
then

Hertzmark
>then

Ruby
>and this is dreadful
>suddenly
>I begin to scream (*does, between* ...)
>a fearful scream of despair
>that rises up from the bottomless loch
>deep inside me
>a place with neither
>name
>number
>nor end ...
>
>The water ...
>The water!!!!

Hertzmark
>What's in the water, Ruby?

Patricia
>I know! ... Ruby! ...

Ruby
>But the wind carries away the rest of her words ...
>and Mr Stewart
>with great difficulty
>turns the boat round
>and heads back to the shelter of the harbour ...
>
>and from then on
>the only events are ...

Patricia
>George comes across
>Mr Roper copulating with our mother
>on the dark oak of the guest house
>dining-room table ...

George
 Whore!

Ruby
 and . . .

Bunty
 Stand up straight, Patricia.

Patricia
 Actually, Mama . . . I just came down to tell you I'm pregnant.

Ruby
 Can anyone top that?

Mrs Roper
 Help! Help!
 Somebody call an ambulance!
 Christine's appendix is bursting!

Nell
 Look at you standing in all this beautiful corn, Lillian!

Ruby
 And then it's Homeward Bound

Bunty
 And No Noise In The Back!

Patricia (*whispering*)
 Do you remember
 Auntie Doreen?

Ruby
 Of course I do.

 Both sigh . . .

 Bunty has given Rags to the RSPCA
 He is about to go to the electric chamber
 when we come back.

Rags yapping and tail-wagging . . .

Patricia
I bought him back with my own pocket money.

Bunty and Patricia stare at each other with hatred . . .

Ruby
So only Patricia gets a holiday
that year . . .

Patricia
I'm going to stay in a Methodist
mother-and-baby-home . . .
Lucky or what?

Ruby
When she comes back . . .
a mother-and-no-baby . . .
she was a different person
somehow . . .

Sad music . . .

Do you want a piece of
toffee, Patricia?

Patricia
No.

Ruby
Shall we go to a film?

Patricia
No, thank you.

Ruby
Patricia never went back to school
never took her A-levels
she was so full of darkness . . .

Patricia
> You'll look after Rags, won't you,
> Ruby?

Ruby
> That in some awful way
> it was a relief when she walked out
> one bright May morning
> and never came home again . . .

Music . . . sort of Waltzing Matilda . . . ? Wild Colonial Boy?

As Patricia walks off . . . into Lillian, dressed for travel . . . suitcase . . . baby . . .

Nell
> Lillian?
> Where are you?

Lillian
> Well, here's my bonny lad.
> We're going to emigrate!

Booking Clerk
> How far are you going Miss?

Lillian
> All the way please.

Nell
> It might be something if you knew
> who the father is . . .

Lillian
> I know who his father is.

Nell
> Who?
>
> Who?

Ruby
   . . . and Grandma . . .
   after Patricia goes . . .
   she pops her clogs too.

Nell
   I'm very disappointed with life.

   Lillian?

Ruby
   Patricia?

Lillian (*failing to write*)
   Dear Nell . . .
   How are you . . . ?

   I am doing well.
   Wide open spaces.   Heat.
   Don't worry about me.

Nell
   Well, here I am.
   Out of it.
   Mother?

   Light fades . . .

SIXTEEN
WEDDING BELLS: 1966

Ruby
   I miss the Pets.
   there's a high snigger factor to
   everything we carry . . .
   not just the contraceptives . . .
   but the shelves of incontinence pads . . .
   prosthetic breasts like small
   conical sandbags . . .

trusses   colostomy bags
and this month's special offer . . .
thick rubber sheeting . . .
it smells like car tyres . . .

Hertzmark
Above the Shop
has never been right since the Fire.

Ruby
I know it's just a trick of
lath and plaster and light . . .
but sometimes . . .
if I stand on the stairs
and close my eyes . . .
I can hear the household ghosts . . .

Hertzmark
Do they miss you?

now you're in the semi . . .

A phone rings . . .

Bunty
Hello . . . this is the Lennox Residence
how can I help you?

Hello?
Hello?
Mr Nobody again.

Ruby (*whispers*)
Patricia?
Patricia?

Bunty
Tie. You. Hurry.

George
Ruby!   Are you going to this
wedding????

Bunty
>Oh for heaven's sake!
>She's the *bridesmaid*!

George
>*You?*

Ruby
>Me.

George
>What's the date?

Bunty
>Next Saturday.

George
>But that's . . .

Commentary
>'. . . the final of the 1966 World Cup . . .
>between England and Germany . . . '

Ruby
>And so here we are at the wedding
>
>*Wedding scene configures around her . . .*
>
>The bridesmaids . . . in pale peach
>polyester satin dresses, like
>the bride's – big round, puffy dresses
>with big round puffy sleeves . . . our
>satin slippers dyed to match our
>dresses, as are our carnatian posies
>and on our heads we wear artificial
>peach-coloured rosebuds on vice-like
>Alice-bands are
>me
>and Daisy and Rose . . .
>the twins from outer space . . .

Twins
So, Ruby?

Ruby
Hello, Rose, how are you?

Daisy
I'm Daisy, actually, Ruby.

Ruby
You've got the freckle. I can see it.

Twins
Enjoying being a bridesmaid, Ruby?

Ruby
It's alright.

Twins
Of course, people feel sorry for you.
I expect that's why they chose you.

Losing so many sisters.

To lose one sister might be
considered careless . . .

But to lose three . . .
well . . . that's a bit suspicious
don't you think
Ruby?

Goodness, Ruby, what on earth
do you do with them all?

Ruby
Two sisters.
I only have two sisters
and Patricia isn't lost
she's coming back

Twins
Don't be so sure.

Ruby
>When I get married . . .
>the church will be illuminated
>by banks of tall white candles
>
>my antique lace dress will fall in
>drifts of snow . . .
>the wedding ceremony concludes . . .

Bunty
>Well, at least no one fell over . . .

Ruby
>and then it's the reception . . .
>
>*Wedding hubbub* . . .

George
>Is there a TV Lounge?
>The Game must have started!

Commentary
>And it's Ball with the corner
>Hurst . . . a chance at goal . . .
>
>It's all smiles in the Royal Box . . .
>
>And it's a free kick to West Germany . . .
>One minute to go, just sixty seconds . . .
>
>Every Englishman coming back . . .
>Every German going forward . . .

Ruby
>It's a buffet do.

Bunty
>It can't hold a candle to a real
>sitdown do . . .

Guest
>I remember Linda's do . . .

Guest 2
   roast topside and all the trimmings.

Guest 3
   They could at least have had a
   proper York Ham . . .

Ruby
   Soon everybody's at least three
   double gins the worse for wear . . .

   Wedding hubbub button to 'max' . . .

   I'm looking forward
   to the relative calm of the TV Lounge . . .
   at first I'm not sure what I'm seeing . . .

   It's a struggling black-and-white heap in the middle of the floor . . .

   and then I get it . . .
   it's George in black tie . . .
   and the buffet waitress in her
   black dress and white apron
   and they're . . .
   having sex . . .

George
   Oh yes oh yes . . .
   (*coming*) Oh bloody, bloody Norah!!!!

   He collapses in a sated heap on top of her . . .

   I want to ask her if by any chance
   she really *is* called Nora . . .

   Waitress catches Ruby's eye and starts struggling . . .
   she rolls George off her . . .

   He lies
   not moving

She starts doing up her clothing . . . her eyes fixed like Ruby's on his lifeless form . . .

The realisation dawns at exactly
the same moment for us.

They drop to their knees on either side of him.

TV Commentary
This great moment in sporting
history . . . as Bobby Moore goes
up to get the World Cup . . .

Waitress
He's not breathing . . .

Ruby
No.

Waitress
He's dead.

Ruby
Yes.

Waitress
Do you know who he is?

Ruby
He's my father.

Waitress gives a yelp.

Waitress
Yiiiipppe!

Don't usually do this sort of thing.

Ruby
I don't know whether she
means casual sex . . .
or inadvertently killing them off . . .

Someone calls Bunty

Bunty
What's matter?
Dead drunk?

Ruby
We think he's had a heart attack.

Bunty
Call an ambulance . . .

Waitress
It's too late for that.

(*tenderly*) Did you know him?

Bunty
He's my husband.

Waitress gives another yelp . . .

Waitress
Yiiippppe!!!

I'll get an ambulance.

Bunty
We have to do something!

She leans over drunkenly . . . and starts to give George artificial respiration . . .

Ruby
It's the first time I've seen them kiss.
She kisses him with all the passion
of a new bride.
It's too late.
He's dead.

Commentary continues . . . into

Funeral music . . .

SEVENTEEN
MISUNDERSTOOD

Ruby
My funeral is a very moving
occasion.
My coffin rests in the aisle of
a beautiful old church
my raven hair has grown
longer, darker, more luxuriant . . .
and I'm surrounded by grieving mourners

In hushed, reverent whispers . . .

Mourner 1
She was so beautiful

Mourner 2
and so misunderstood . . .

Mourner 3
if only we had realized how
incredibly special she was

Mourner 4
and don't forget talented

Bunty
Perhaps if she hadn't been swapped
at birth this would never have happened

. . . but I don't think you were

Hertzmark
swapped at birth, were you?

Ruby
No

Hertzmark
    And you are still alive aren't you?

Ruby
    Yes.

Hertzmark
    and
    you know
    you are beautiful
    and incredibly special
    and talented
    and misunderstood . . .

Ruby
    Yes.

Hertzmark
    and
    I think your hair is fine as it is . . .
    so
    now
    tell me more . . .

EIGHTEEN
A NEW SUITOR

Ruby
    Bunty wastes no time getting
    back into the swing of things
    Romance-wise

Bunty
    Your father's friend Bernard
    Belling is *such* a gentleman . . .

    Bernard appears . . .

Ruby
> He has a plumbing business somewhere
> in the nether regions of Back Swinegate . . .

> *Sanitary, lavatorial sounds (refined) . . .*

Bunty
> His warehouse is like a cathedral
> dedicated to sanitary ware . . .
> lidless toilets gleam . . .
> stacks of tapless sinks . . .

Bernard
> Your poor mother's had a wretched life . . .

Bunty
> Bernard . . .

Bernard
> How long until you leave home then, Ruby?

Bunty
> Kathleen's your age and she's got
> a steady boyfriend and is saving up
> for her bottom drawer!
> She's a very sensible girl.

Ruby
> You don't want me to go to
> university then?

Bernard (*attitude*)
> University!

Bunty
> Yes, yes, of course I do.
> Your education's very important,
> obviously.

Bernard (*attitude*)
> Education!

Ruby
>She really wants me to get married
>and belong to someone *else*!

Bernard
>Who'd take her on?
>I'd take *you* on!

Bunty
>*Bernard!*

Ruby
>What's the point of a bottom drawer?

Bunty
>To save things for the future.

Ruby
>What would I put in
>my bottom drawer?
>
>Something
>
>just out of my reach
>
>hidden on a high shelf
>
>under a floorboard.
>
>There is the key
>
>What will the key open?

Hertzmark
>And this is where you start going mad . . .
>
>*Noise: traffic, confusion of earlier sounds as . . .*

Bunty
>She walked right out of school
>she was supposed to be in *Latin*!
>She nearly got run down in
>Clifton Green!

Man
>You stupid bloody girl!
>Why don't you look where you're going?

Bernard
>Ruby!
>What on earth are you doing girl?

Ruby
>Trying to escape!

Bunty
>Just ignore her, Bernard
>She's too clever for her own good
>She takes after her sister

Ruby
>Which one of the many
>children you've lost
>would that be?

Bernard slaps Ruby across the face.

Bunty
>Thank you Bernard . . .
>Long past time somebody put
>*you* in your place, milady.
>Shall I open a tin of salmon?

Ruby
>What would I put in my bottom drawer?
>
>Only sharp objects . . .
>clean lines of broken glass
>honed steel of paring knives
>soothing edges of razor blades . . .

Bernard
>Why don't you offer me a little
>drink, Ruby?

Ruby
   Why don't you get it yourself?

Bernard
   What a rude little madam you are.

Ruby
   And I don't like you either.

Bernard
   You're going to get what's
   coming to you one of these days
   Ruby Lennox . . .

Ruby
   Oh yeah . . . what's that . . .
   love and affection?

Bernard
   Your poor mother's given
   you everything but you're
   just an ungrateful little bitch!

Ruby
   You don't know anything!

Bernard
   You killed your own sister, Ruby!
   You killed your own sister!
   I ask you . . .
   what kind of a little girl
   would do that?

Bunty (*off*)
   Are you ready, Bernard?
   It's curtain up at half past seven!

Bernard
   I know all about you, Ruby . . .
   Your mother told me everything!

Ruby
>I did not kill my sister!
>She was run over!

Bernard
>I don't mean that one
>you stupid little girl
>I mean your twin sister!

Bunty (*off*)
>Bernard!
>We're off to the theatre now
>Ruby . . .
>
>we'll see you later!

Hertzmark
>And you . . .

Ruby
>Run upstairs to Bunty's bedroom . . .
>and poke about on the top shelf
>of her fitted wardrobe in which
>she keeps the shoe-box
>the one she keeps crammed with
>the bits of paper that make our
>lives official and random objects
>that can't find a home anywhere
>else but somehow cannot be
>thrown away . . .
>I sift my way down
>through the medical cards
>log books
>insurance certificates,
>a broken earring
>an old ration book
>a silver locket
>mortgage papers
>a mouldy-looking paw

an old theatre programme
a plastic ring from a cracker

After a while
I get down to George's will
and death certificate
Bunty and George's marriage certificate
Gillian's death certificate
and then all the birth certificates
held together with a rubber band . . .
Berenice Eileen
George Arthur
Patricia Vivian
Gillian Berenice
Ruby Eleanor

And Pearl's.

There I have it.
Pearl.

Pearl Ada Lennox

Born in Fulford Maternity Hospital
on
incredibly
the same day
of the same month
of the same year as

me.
The 8th of February 1952.

She reads it over and over again and compares it, looking from one to the other endlessly as if eventually they would explain themselves.

There is only one explanation

Pearl Ada Lennox really was
my twin sister.

A dreadful, threatening pulse beating in her stomach.

Yet I have no recollection
of this sister!

I have a strange surge of memory
as if caught in a photographer's flash

Flash . . .

of alphabet cards in a horseshoe.

perhaps
like Elvis's twin
Pearl died at birth.

Perhaps
we were Siamese twins
and she had to die for me to live!

That's what Mr Belling meant!

But somehow
I didn't think so.

I rake down through the papers
in the shoeless shoebox

*She does . . . until finally right down at the bottom
she finds what she is looking for*

Another death certificate.

(*reads*) 'Pearl Ada Lennox.
2nd of January 1956 . . .
Cause of Death . . . drowning . . . '

Sound of water becomes stronger . . .

Why have we never talked about this?

Bunty
You forgot.

Ruby
>I *forgot*! What do you mean 'I forgot'?

Bunty
>You blacked it all out.
>Amnesia.
>Dr Haddow said that was probably for
>the best . . . after what happened.
>We all thought it was for the best.
>After all, nobody wanted to be
>reminded about what happened . . .

Ruby
>But you can't just blot something
>like that out!
>You can't just pretend somebody
>never existed.
>Not talk about them!
>Not look at photographs . . .

Bunty
>There *are* photographs.
>and of course we talked about her . . .
>it was you that blotted her out
>not us.

Ruby (*screams*)
>It's always *my* fault, isn't it?
>
>How did I kill my sister?

Bunty
>You pushed her in the water.
>
>It was an accident

Ruby
>An accident?
>
>Bernard Belling talked about it as
>if I was a coldblooded murderer . . .

Bunty
> Well, he shouldn't have been
> talking to you about it . . .
>
> At the time, I did blame you
> but of course it *was* an accident . . .

Bunty
> You didn't know it would happen
> you were only five years old
>
> It was a long time ago
>
> There's no point bringing it up again

Ruby
> Show me the locket
>
> *All the ghosts attend . . .*
>
> Which one?   Which one is Pearl?

Bunty
> This one. On the left. My Pearl.

Ruby
> Pearl.
>
> And then blackness

Hertzmark
> Ten
> nine
> eight
> seven
> six
> five
> four
> three
> two
> one . . .

NINETEEN
2 JANUARY 1956: ELVINGTON

Memory music . . .

Ruby
After Christmas . . .
January . . .
we went to visit Uncle Tom and
Auntie Mabel at Elvington . . .
Bunty . . . George . . . Patricia . . . Gillian
me . . . and . . . and . . .

Ruby (*very painful*)
. . . Pearl . . .

George
I thought the roads might be blocked.
it was a real white-over last night!

Ruby
Auntie Mabel gives us a tongue salad

Gillian
I like this.
Why can't we have this?
What is it?

Bunty
Tongue, Gillian.

Gillian
Tongue. Tongue. Tongue.
(*realisation*) . . . *Tongue!!!*

Patricia
Hahaha . . .

Ruby
And Pearl laughs too Pearl

likes to laugh she's all light and sunshine
to my dark . . .

Bunty
That's enough laughing thank you . . .

George
You can play in the snow after dinner . . .
We put your wellingtons in the boot . . .

Ruby
And Pearl says . . .
can we make a big snowman?
and I say . . . can we take some
coal from the scuttle for his eyes?
That's enough!

Hertzmark
No
keep going, Ruby . . .

Ruby
Bunty and Aunt Mabel
are buttoning us into our duffel
coats . . . Pearl and I have little
woollen bonnets . . .
mine is red
hers is blue
with little white pompoms on top.
Pearl is so excited by the snow . . .
she paddles her feet up and down . . .

Bunty
Stand *still*, Pearl!

Ruby
We stream out into the cold . . .
Patricia   Gillian   Pearl   and me
our voices ringing like bells in
the clear air . . .

Bunty
>Mind you don't go near the duck pond!

Ruby
>She might as well have said

Bunty
>Mind you go straight to the duck pond!

Patricia
>Let's go to the duck pond!

Ruby
>It's a . . .

Patricia
>Magical place!

Ruby
>A frozen ice-scape of sparkling white . . .
>snow-covered trees on the . . .

Gillian (*very excited*)
>. . . island in the middle!

Ruby
>The duck pond is so full of
>winter water . . . it's flooded out onto
>the field . . . you can look through
>the glassy ice and
>see the green grass below

A sound of geese cackling . . .

Patricia
>Oh, we should have brought some bread!

Ruby
>Gillian finds a sheet of solid ice
>and bangs her foot like a demented Disney

Ruby
Rabbit!

Gillian
Hurray! Hurray!

Patricia
Be *careful*, Gillian!

Ruby
Pearl runs after Gillian . . .
she jumps up and down as she watches
her sister perform the miracle of
walking on water . . .

Gillian
I'm walking on water . . .
I'm walking on water to
the island! . . .

A sound of great ice cracking . . .

Gillian laughing . . .

Ruby
Pearl has got both feet on the ice!

Gillian (*laughing, shouting*)
Come on!
Come on, don't be a coward!
Cowardy-custard Pearl!

Ruby (*voice-over*)
Because she knows that's the
one way to goad Pearl into doing
things . . . (*end voice-over*) Pearl . . . come back!

Gillian
Shut up, Ruby!
You're just a big baby!

Patricia
   I'm behind a clump of trees!
   With the *geese*!

Ruby
   So Patricia doesn't see
   Pearl has walked nearly half way
   across the ice!
   I can see it moving!
   Slight seesaw motion!

   Ice creaks . . .

Gillian
   Come on, come on Pearl!

Ruby
   Then
   then
   then
   the ice   tilts
   and   she slides off as if she's
   been tipped on a chute
   and   she slips into the water
   quite slowly and
   feet first
   and
   as she drops into the water
   she twists round so she's facing me
   and the last thing I see is her face . . .

Gillian
   Patricia! Hurry up!

   Quacking of geese . . . terribly loud . . .

Patricia
   No! No! No!

Ruby
her face . . .
stretched in   horror!
and the last words she ever says . . .

Gillian
Patricia! In the water!

Patricia
I dive
Again
and again
and again
but

Ruby
before the black water claims her
hang on the freezing air
forming ice-crystals of sound
long after the little white pompom on
her hat has disappeared . . .

Patricia
I can't find her!
I look
and look
and look
but

Ruby
all I can really hear are Pearl's
words
which have found a home inside my skull
creating
dreadful
ricocheting echoes

Pearl (*little girl's voice*)
    Ruby, help me!
    Ruby, help me!

Ruby
    Grown-ups come
    they drag Patricia screaming and
    kicking from the pond . . .

Patricia
    No! She's in there! Pearl's *in* there!

Ruby
    Gillian's stranded on the island
    a little rowing boat gets her off . . .

Gillian
    It was her, it was her, it was her.
    Ruby pushed her in
    she pushed Pearl in the water . . .
    I saw her!
    I saw her!

Ruby
    And my heart   breaks!

An awful sound of ice cracking and breaking . . .

Great   jagged   icy splinters

She takes great noisy gulps of air.

I'm drowning on air!
and   if I could cast a spell to stop time
suspend it for ever and ever
so cobwebs grew in my hair
ducks stopped in their circles
feathers lay still on the air
drifting through time for ever
I would do it.

Hertzmark
　Alright?

Ruby
　No.

Hertzmark
　Here.
　Have a Lyons chocolate cupcake.

Ruby
　My mother really did blame me.
　She packed me off to her sister
　in Dewsbury.
　She couldn't bear to look at me.

Hertzmark
　Because you reminded her of Pearl . . .
　not because she hated you.

Ruby
　Both, I suppose.
　Poor Bunty. Losing two children.
　And Patricia too.
　We expected her to save Pearl
　And she couldn't.

Surprises herself with . . .

　And poor Gillian too.
　If anyone was to blame　　it was her.
　And she's dead.
　And poor Pearl
　because she's dead too.

Hertzmark
　And so . . .
　Shall we go through every person
　in the world
　dead or alive

and say 'poor so and so'
and 'poor so and so'
and will we ever come to
'poor Ruby'?

Ruby
Poor Ruby

The words have hardly formed in her mouth before she is crying and crying . . .

Poor Ruby

I have been to the world's end
and back
I know what I would put in my bottom drawer.

I would put my sisters.

Beautiful music . . .

EPILOGUE

Ruby
I took a train.
Edinburgh
in an Italian café off Leith Walk
behind the counter
is a beautiful boy with green eyes
this is Gian-Carlo Benedetti . . .
and one night when the café is closed
he proposes to me over a seething
cup of cappucino in dreadful
halting English
I condemn myself to
some truly wretched years in
which Gian-Carlo's charms melt
into the air along with his fine

cheek bones and radiant smile . . .
but

I give birth to my two
nutbrown girls

my twins

The locket appears . . . two bonny girls in it . . .

and then
I have to come back to York
my mother's dying . . .

Intensive care hospital ward configures around her . . .

I'm waiting for Bunty to die
with Sister Blake . . .

Sister Blake attends . . .

and someone comes in.
Perhaps it will be Mr Nobody.
It's not.

Patricia
Mother?
Ruby?
Is that you, Ruby?

Ruby
Patricia.

From Australia

Return of Australian Waltzing Matilda / Wild Colonial Boy music . . .

Into . . .

Sounds of hospital . . .

Patricia
How did she shrink so much?

Ruby
> I don't think I've ever looked
> at my mother so much as this night . . .

Sister Blake
> She's hanging by a thread . . .

Ruby
> Now I come to study her
> I feel I have no idea who she is . . .

Sister Blake
> I think she's taken a turn for the worse.
>
> I never knew my real mother.
> I was adopted.
> Not knowing your real mother
> nags at you,
> you know?

Patricia
> Didn't you try to find her?

Sister Blake
> Oh yes, but she was dead by then.
> She came from Belfast
> that's all I know about her . . .

Ruby
> What about your father?

Sister Blake
> Canadian apparently.
> RAF.
> Died. War you know.
>
> *Edmund appears . . .*

Edmund
> Hi!
> Doreen!
> Can I stay the night?

Bunty
   Edmund?
   Edmund!

Sister Blake
   I think she's gone!

Bunty joins Edmund. She is radiant.

Ruby
   I'd expected some
   meaningful last words
   pearls of wisdom
   a deathbed confession . . .

   I am not your real mother!

   but

Patricia
   Well, that's over with.

Ruby
   Nothing
   not even goodbye.

Patricia
   We loved her really.

Ruby
   It's not what I'd call love.

Patricia
   Maybe not, but it's love all the same.

Ruby
   We're outside now.
   There's a dark, star-studded sky.
   We start walking up the hill . . .

Patricia
   I don't think the dead are lost

for ever anyway,
do you, Ruby?

Ruby
Nothing's lost for ever, Patricia.
It's all there somewhere.
Every last pin.

Patricia
Pin?

Ruby
Believe me, Patricia.
I've been to the end of the world.
I know what happens.

Patricia
The past is what you leave behind
in life, Ruby.

Ruby
Nonsense, Patricia,
the past's what you take with you.

The breeze turns suddenly chilly. They both turn up their coat collars

Ruby puts her arm in Patricia's.

the past is a cupboard full of light
and all you have to do is find the
key that opens the door . . .

Music.

Stars twinkle and shine . . . then

Darkness

Then . . .

The End.